Light Body Human Universal

An Adaptationist View of Non-Newtonian Anatomy

E. Stephens Gain

Spinguin Media

This book was written by a human.
Copyright © 2025 E. Stephens Gain

All rights reserved.

No part of this book may be reproduced, stored in a retrieval system, or transmitted in any form or by any means, electronic, mechanical, photocopying, recording, or otherwise, without express written permission of the author.

No part of this book may be used to train an artificial intelligence system of any kind.

Like the punk-rock zines of yore that were duplicated with a copy machine, this book is published in small print-to-order runs. Irregularities in printing should be cherished as character embellishments of a human-produced product.

Spinguin Media
Grass Valley, CA

Bookstore inquiries: books@spinguin.com

Paperback ISBN: 979-8-9989868-8-8
Hardback ISBN: 979-8-9989868-6-4
Kindle ISBN: 979-8-9989868-2-6
ePub ISBN: 979-8-9989868-0-2

For Don Symons. I know you'd be proud.

Contents

Preface
1 - What this book is and Who it is for   1

PART I - PERCEPTION & KNOWING

2 - Introducing the Light Body   7
    The Stephens Gain Theorem   10
3 - Lessons In Knowing   16
    Remote Viewing   19
4 - No Time For Skeptics   30

PART II - LIGHT BODY THEORY

5 - Light Body Theory   35
6 - Using Human Universals Theory   40
    Emic and Etic   41
7 - Mental Mechanisms & Variability   43
8 - Evidence for the Light Body   50
9 - Light Body is Energy with Adaptation   59
10 - Earthization   67
11 - A Summary   70

PART III - A MODEL OF THE LIGHT BODY

12 - A Theoretical Model   77
13 - How do we Move our Light Bodies?   80
14 - Light Body Behaviors   87
15 - Light Body Memory and Homeostasis   93
16 - Social Intelligence   98
17 - Light Body is Free from the Now Moment 108
    Extension Transfers and Psi Research   112
18 - Recording Technology   116
    Light Language in Recorded Media 120

Part IV - APPLYING LIGHT BODY THEORY

19 - How to Use This Book   127
20 - Evolutionary Match   128
    Friendship and Safety   129
    Cultural Transmission   129
    Cooperation   130
    Coalitions   131
    Cults   132
21 - Evolutionary Mismatch   136
    Reading   137
    The Printing Press   140
    Light Body Development & Technology   141
    The Internet and Smartphones   144
22 - What Could Go Wrong?   146
    Mind-machine Interfaces   146
    Russia   149
    AI Interfaces   153
    Social Media   160
23 - Going Forward   162
    For Teachers   162
    For Media Producers   162
    For Religion Scholars   164
    For Healthcare Professionals   165
    For Scientists and Tech Developers   167
    For Lightworkers   164

APPENDICES

Introduction to Channeled Literature   171
A Light Language Demonstration   174
References   176
Index   183
Glossary   186
Acknowledgements   188

Preface

> "My role in society, or any artist's or poet's role, is to try and express what we all feel. Not to tell people how to feel. Not as a preacher, not as a leader, but as a reflection of us all."
>
> ~ *John Lennon*

I feel my Light Body.

I feel it inside and extending beyond my regular body, filling the space around me like an invisible egg.

I feel when my Light Body overlaps with someone else's Light Body.

My Light Body feels like an antenna when I'm in a group of people and when I move from one place to another.

I feel my Light Body respond when I'm exposed to art or music.

I feel my Light Body interface with my emotions and my physical body.

I feel my Light Body sway with the ebb and flow of some sort of invisible "space weather."

None of this makes me special. Everyone has a Light Body, and lots of people can feel their Light Bodies too.

What is special about me is that I have studied lots of different approaches to learn what I can do with my Light Body. I was originally trained to do mainstream research in biology and experimental psychology. I have extensive experience with non-traditional wisdom sources including channeling and channeled literature, energetic healing, and a variety of religious and new age practices. I left academia 26 years ago, but a scientific perspective deeply informs my thought processes as I move among different metaphysical worlds.

I am rare among scientists because my pandemic project obliged me to "come out" publicly as someone who feels their Light Body. When the world shut down in 2020, I created a website to deep dive into metaphysical exploration with a large group of people all over the world who "Work With I Am the Word." I am grateful for their support of my curiosity.

Throughout hundreds of Zoom sessions, I definitively learned that people from all walks of life feel their Light Bodies too. One thing we have in common is that we're used to catering to people who don't feel their Light Bodies (or pretend they don't feel them). I don't do that anymore, so that won't happen here.

When the world re-opened, I met scientists, often former classmates and colleagues, who were fascinated by my pandemic project and wanted to know what I had learned. Many of them craved validation for their own experiences, so I gave demos and developed an online class just for them. Writing this book is the logical next step.

The contents of this book are a synthesis of my ideas based on 30 years of meditative consciousness experimentation (i.e. without drugs). I've integrated and organized ideas from biology, anthropology, psychology, and channeled literature[1] into what I call "Light Body Theory." In the same way that Temple Grandin's books illuminate the reality and utility of visual thinking, it's my intention that this book will validate a new variety of inner experience that serves "as a reflection of us all."

---

[1] See the Appendix "Introduction to Channeled Literature" if you're unfamiliar with it.

It's my belief that Light Body Theory is urgently needed to help us understand and deal with current events in the United States and around the globe. The runaway influence of new technology on society and politics is a crisis that warrants consideration of unconventional solutions. I hope to find readers who are equally motivated to address this crisis.

E. Stephens Gain
Grass Valley, California
July 1, 2025

Do you feel your Light Body too? I'd love to hear from you and to know your reasons for reading this book. Send me an email at *hello@TriforiumTribune.com*.

Also, I've made a reading list for people unfamiliar with the references cited in this book. If that's you, then you can subscribe to my Substack, *Expanded Consciousness 101*. This free newsletter is a 12-month literary survey about consciousness science and channeling. When you subscribe, the syllabus will be emailed to you, and monthly emails include short book reviews and links to related media to get you up to speed. There's a link to subscribe on TriforiumTribune.com.

CHAPTER ONE

What this book is and Who it is for

People in the United States today live in two different worlds. Our inner world is a stream of consciousness full of ideas, feelings, imagination, and sensation. It's real. It's private, and we're free to choose how to make our lives meaningful. The outer world of society, however, has rules about what we can say is "real." We all know that if you break those rules, you'll be ostracized and called crazy.

People do more than what society's rules about reality allow. We move through our days following our unspoken intuition, our gut feelings. We use music and sound to change how our body feels. We use Reiki and Qi Gong to change how our body heals. We experience synchronicities that change what we know about our place in the world or about our connectedness to other people. We become aware of information that we could not have perceived through any of our "normal" senses. We experience it in our inner world, so we know it's real and it changes our lives, even though it defies what is supposed to be possible.

This book is my attempt to change the rules about reality so they better reflect human potential. I'm normalizing expanded consciousness for people in the United States and other cultures that share our worldview because of our common descent from the Holy Roman Empire.

This book is for scientists and academics who are frustrated with the traditional materialist paradigm about consciousness. Most of you are neck deep in the environment that makes the rules, and you're surrounded by people invested in maintaining what came before them. Many of you practice subtle energy techniques or learn from channeled wisdom sources in secret. Some of you have tried hallucinogenics and want help incorporating new truths into your daily lives. Some of you embrace religion as a comforting, time-tested source of guidance for inner navigation, while others are "spiritual but not religious" because you've learned to trust your own knowing in private. I can provide you with a breath of fresh air that will validate your experience and support you to keep exploring.

On a practical level, this book is also for my work with K-12 teachers. I teach teachers to use subtle energy techniques for stress management in the classroom. Teachers are warriors who enter the fray every single day, and they need strategies to support their stamina. They don't have time for mainstream science to catch up and tell them what works. With this book, I hope to create a scientific theoretical foundation that legitimizes doing subtle energy work in public spaces like schools.

There is another, more speculative reason for this book. I believe I may have discovered a new way to influence society through media manipulation. I call myself a "Light Language Recording Artist" (a term I invented) because I want to make people aware of this phenomenon. As far-fetched as it may seem, I am concerned about potential influence by a foreign country where research on expanded consciousness seems to be more encouraged than it is here. You guessed it, it's Russia.

What this book is and Who it is for

The content within this book is based on my own exploration of consciousness and my studies of evolutionary biology, evolutionary psychology, and biological anthropology. It is also based on my superficial understanding of modern theoretical physics and my faith that physicists have actually figured out something for us to build on.

It's as short and as easy to read as I could make it. I'm doing my best not to waste your time.

There is homework. There are four articles that you'll need to find online and devote some time to reading. (At least read the abstracts and skim the rest.) I've put links to them on my website at TriforiumTribune.com, or you can look them up yourself with the citations. There is also instruction to take a break from reading in Chapter Three and try something new. Please do your homework. You will learn much more from the original sources and from your own doing than you can learn from me.

This book is divided into four parts.

Part I establishes that expanded consciousness is normal. I offer ideas and suggest experiences to ease you into accepting a greater version of human potential than is popularly acknowledged. I want you to self-identify with your Light Body in a very real way.

Part II is the meat and potatoes of Light Body Theory. This is the main entrée that you'll need to digest in order to understand the greater implications of what's happening here.

Part III is where I show you what it's like to be me. I analyze my practical experience of the Light Body to build a model based on the principles of evolution. Once you get it, you'll see that applying Light Body Theory illuminates a myriad of mysteries. This is just the beginning.

If you keep turning pages, eventually you'll make it to **Part IV**, which is the monster at the end of this book.[2] I'll discuss the many ways our Light Bodies are involved in modern society, including our relationship with technology. We'll look at the possibility that our societal ignorance of Light Body Intelligence might make us vulnerable to exploitation by foreign powers hostile to the United States (Russia). I'll also give advice for adopting Light Body Theory within different professional fields.

If you're the type of reader who loves a shortcut, you're probably already considering jumping ahead to Part IV. The shortest shortcut I recommend is:

> 1 - The Stephens Gain Theorem info-graphic in Chapter 2
> 2 - Chapter 6 - Using Human Universals Theory
> 3 - Chapter 7 - Mental Mechanisms & Variability
> 4 - Chapter 10 - Earthization
> 5 - Part IV - Applying Light Body Theory

Here's an even shorter suggestion. I've been told that Chapter 21: Evolutionary Mismatch is the best chapter in this book. So read that chapter, then use the table of contents to hunt down the things you didn't understand.

Read on intrepid reader, read on.

---

[2] A reference to Grover from Sesame Street, as told in *The Monster At the End of This Book* by Jon Stone & Mike Smolin, illustrator, 1971, Little Golden Books.

Part One

Perception & Knowing

E. Stephens Gain

CHAPTER TWO

Introducing the Light Body

This chapter welcomes you to the realm of intellectual nerdery, so first let's give thanks to the ancestors. All who read this book are descended from an unbroken lineage of philosopher scientists ignited with curiosity to decipher how humans work. I'm grateful for those who delighted in their discoveries as we do today. Our work is an endless exploration to reveal all we can do with our temporary human lives.

For half a century, the cultures descended from Western Europe have been dominated by one philosophical style. René Descartes was its most famous champion, so it's called *Cartesian Dualism*. It's the idea that the mind and the body are two different substances. For the most part, this approach has enabled great progress in science and technology. It's deeply instilled in our society. It's an invisible belief we all agree to respect.

In the past century, however, people began to seek philosophies that enabled them to use more of their human potential. A myriad of pioneering explorers discovered that we don't need to limit ourselves with Cartesian Dualism. Groups gathered to develop healing methods and ways of accessing information beyond our known physical senses (e.g. Mesmerism and Western Mysticism).

Many in the United States welcomed ancient wisdom traditions (e.g. Rosicrucians, Kaballah, Sikhism) and embraced the anatomy philosophies of foreign cultures (e.g. Yoga, Chinese medicine, Qi Gong, Ayurveda). By the late 20th century, mainstream scientists were producing data that proved Cartesian Dualism wrong (e.g. Robert Jahn and Brenda Dunne[3] of the Princeton Engineering Anomalies Research lab, William Tiller[4] of Stanford Materials Science and Engineering, and NASA astronaut Edgar Mitchell [5]who founded the Institute for Noetic Sciences).

There is ever-growing support to adopt a more expansive world view, yet it has not had an effect on our cultural norms. Most people use language that keeps everyone comfortable with what we've known. Terms like "Alternative Medicine" give credence to greater truths, while still putting them outside the boundary of mainstream acceptance. The word "placebo" is used by those stuck in the purgatory of Cartesian Dualism as a way to dismiss data that defies explanation. More and more, scientist philosophers argue against "materialism," but no one listens. It's the norm to unquestionably accept "the brain" as a synonym for "the mind," as the source of all ideas and intelligence. The truth is that no one has a definitive answer to explain where ideas come from.

MY WORLD VIEW

I was educated in Biology and Experimental Psychology, so I used to feel obliged to adhere to materialism[6] for fear of ridicule, yet it

---

[3] Dunne, Brenda and Jahn, Robert, eds. (2017). *Being and Biology: Is Consciousness the Life Force?* ICRL Press.
[4] Tiller, William. (1997). *Science and Human Transformation: Subtle Energies, Intentionality and Consciousness.* Pavior Publishing.
[5] Mitchell, Edgar D. (1974). *Psychic Exploration: a challenge for Science.* Perigee Books.
[6] Materialism is the outdated paradigm based solely on matter,

was not my truth. As an undergraduate student, I once awakened amazed because during my sleep I had astral traveled around campus and through empty buildings in the dark. That morning, I attended a biology class. I laughed with joy that I was no longer afraid to die while I took lecture notes on theories that had no capacity to explain what I just did. As a Psychology graduate student researching human memory, I did not believe that memories are *stored in the brain* like a computer,[7] yet I cooperated with the institutional norm to accept it as fact. During my time in academia, I had a nagging feeling that most experimental psychologists deluded themselves by ignoring and disparaging well-documented strange phenomena like hypnosis, channeling, and accessing information with *psychic* or *supernatural* talents.

From my perspective, there is no supernatural, and I wish people would stop using that word. It's a term used as an excuse to avoid uncomfortable truths. It locks us into a limited view of reality because people with mainstream success are supposed to reject and ridicule anything that could be described as supernatural.

These were the problems I was tackling when I came up with the idea I'm about to share. I was preparing a presentation for a group of audio recording engineers about what I learned from my pandemic project. I have a lot to say about expanded consciousness and recorded media, but I knew it would be challenging to get them past their initial rejection so we could have a productive discussion. What could I say to get beyond their resistance to new ideas that challenge deep-seated beliefs?

---

electromagnetism, and Classical Physics. It's why we always have to start with brain matter when we discuss consciousness.

[7] I still don't. I believe our brains are recorders and playback devices, but memories are stored in some other-dimensional way we can't comprehend. Akashic Records is a metaphor that's been used throughout history to Earthize this memory store.

WE NEED A NEW EXPRESSION

I created an illustration to simplify the logic of the connections I saw. I came up with a simple mathematical expression to explain my logic, and I presented it at my talk.

I received nods of acceptance, but it didn't have the impact I intended. My audience understood and approved, but it was too much work to think about the implications of the truth I was illuminating, so they just skipped it.

I don't want you to skip it. So, right here, right now, I'm giving this expression a cute info-graphic and a hoity-toity title to inspire you to do the mental work it asks of you. I introduce to you, (dramatic pause)… The Stephens Gain Theorem.

THE STEPHENS GAIN THEOREM

Mainstream knowledge from different academic fields unites to form conclusions that boggle the mind.

Biological Evolution + Non-Newtonian Physics = The Light Body

A theorem is a logical argument that describes a relationship between known facts which produces a truth that is not self-evident on its own.

Let's break down the parts of this theorem. First, the known facts:

Biological Evolution means evolution by natural selection. In simplified terms, it means that human anatomy is the result of complexity that accrued over a long span of time as generations of our species became better at surviving and reproducing. Our evolutionary history has created the adaptive design we see today. This is the most basic principle that informs the fields of

Biology, Medicine, and all humanistic fields including Psychology and Anthropology.

You don't need to understand the complexities of Theoretical Biology to appreciate this fact. If you're doubting what you know about it, I suggest you review the research on Darwin's finches in the Galapagos Islands. Biologists Peter and Rosemary Grant spent 40 years observing the birds' beak and body shape evolve due to changes in the weather and food supply. These are the same birds that inspired Charles Darwin to write *The Origin of Species*, and the Grants have created abundant and clear evidence of evolution by natural selection.[8]

Non-Newtonian Physics is a general term that broadly refers to the past century of progress in the field of Physics, starting with the revolutionary quantum theories of Planck and Einstein. Examples of the science I include in this category are quantum mechanics, entanglement, non-locality, string theory, dark matter, and dark energy.

I lump all these topics together for two reasons. First, it's not necessary to understand physics in order to understand this theorem. The science is mind boggling to most of us, so we just need to trust that the physicists know what they're doing. We're used to trusting physicists because they invented miraculous technologies like cell phones, wifi, quantum computers, and the garage-door remote control. We don't need to understand these technologies to benefit from using them.

Second, I want to emphasize that Non-Newtonian Physics is mysterious and seemingly magical compared to the pre-1900 Classical Physics derived from Isaac Newton's work. Classical Physics describes the "normal" way we observe objects and forces

---

[8] Grant, Peter R.; Grant, B. Rosemary (2014). *40 Years of Evolution: Darwin's Finches on Daphne Major Island*. Princeton University Press.

interacting on a human scale; and the fields of Biology and mainstream Western Medicine are dependent on this way of viewing the world. The "materialist" paradigm is based on Classical Physics.

> "Features of human nature must provide a continuous and pervasive structuring of human thought."
> ~ Donald E. Brown, biological anthropologist and author of *Human Universals*[9]

As this quote from Brown implies, human thought has been structured by evolutionary design. "Newtonian Physics" is merely the subset of all physics properties that our human systems evolved to consciously perceive. Studies with human infants reveal we are born knowing "intuitive physics" to witness the world in a Newtonian way.[10] With this in mind, Isaac Newton was really an Evolutionary Psychologist illuminating features of the human mind.

Non-Newtonian Physics are the physics properties outside the spectrum of physics that our human systems evolved to consciously perceive. That's why they seem magical. Cognitive scientist Donald Hoffman explained this idea with the eloquent phrase, "evolution hid the truth from our eyes." [11]

The Facts reveal The Truth:

The Light Body: With deductive reasoning, the Stephens Gain Theorem justifies the existence of Non-Newtonian adaptations within our human anatomy. I use the term *Light Body* as a shortcut to encapsulate this truth. We don't have to identify or

---

[9] Brown, Donald E. (1991) *Human Universals*. Temple University Press.
[10] Baillargeon, R, Spelke, E, & Wasserman, S. (1985) Object Permanence in five-month-old infants. *Cognition* 20, 191-208.
[11] Hoffman, Donald (2019). *The Case Against Reality.* Penguin Books.

understand the particulars to use this idea. Humans have a Light Body in addition to our Physical Body.

This should seem obvious when I put it this way, but it hasn't been obvious because of the delineations that keep academic fields separate. Modern physicists conduct experiments on Non-Newtonian phenomena with non-biological matter; and modern biologists keep themselves limited to Classical Physics. Natural selection, however, would not have respected these artificial boundaries. Complexity evolved employing Non-Newtonian phenomena within the biological matter of our human anatomy.

Existence of the Light Body should be a mainstream idea. It's my hope that the Stephens Gain Theorem will shake people out of their commitment to uphold the taboo that surrounds consciousness research.

Theorems need to be proved, and this theorem has already been proved with a myriad of experimental approaches including "psi" (a nickname for research on "psychic" or "anomalous" thought), mind-matter research, and research on energy healing and prayer. This is research conducted by reputable scientists affiliated with mainstream institutions. Even the United States government produced a significant amount of proof with their experiments on Remote Viewing, yet they canceled the program because they did not have a way of understanding what their data proved.

The Stephens Gain Theorem defines the Light Body with an Adaptationist Perspective. This is a new scientific way to understand "anomalous cognition" (it doesn't fit) within the traditional materialist paradigm. Light Body Theory in Section II of this book will develop this idea further and outline methods we can use for exploration.

THE STEPHENS GAIN THEOREM INFO-GRAPHIC

The Stephens Gain Theorem

Mainstream knowledge from different academic fields unites to form conclusions that boggle the mind.

Evolution by Natural Selection

Evolution of complexity over a long span of time created anatomy with adaptive design

+

Non-Newtonian Physics

Quantum Mechanics
Entanglement / Non-Locality
String Theory
Unseen Dimensions
Dark Matter / Dark Energy

=

Human Anatomy has Non-Newtonian Adaptations

The Light Body

NEW MYSTERIES TO BE SOLVED

Now that you've made it this far, take a minute to let these ideas really sink in. Acknowledging the Light Body opens the door to a host of thrilling possibilities. Mainstream acceptance of the Light Body is going to change the rules entrenched in societal norms.

As you work your way through the rest of this book, I recommend that you go slowly so you can truly digest this material. This chapter has provided an intellectual understanding of the Light Body (I'll define it in more detail in Chapter 9). The next chapter will guide you to have an experiential understanding of your own Light Body. You'll need to trust both of these knowledge sources in order to make this idea your own. When you do that, you're sure to be inspired. I'm excited to see what you will uncover when you act on your new inspiration.

You and I are a part of the endless progression of human knowledge. We're connected through a lineage lit by curiosity. As you absorb this book, may you experience life instilling joy of intellectual discovery and self-exploration.

CHAPTER THREE

Lessons In Knowing

Chapter Three is a workshop, and you're going to have to do some homework. This chapter will help you see if you're a good fit for the rest of this book.

Most Americans have been trained to internalize skepticism as the right thing to do. We gaslight ourselves, dismissing our personal experiences because we can't satisfy someone else's idea of "proof." In this chapter, I ask you to self-examine your tendency to do that and to learn to trust yourself more.

When you get to the end, I hope you can identify with your own Light Body and your world has become bigger.[12] You're no longer married to materialism as the only take on reality. You're ready to start figuring out what you can do with your Light Body, and Light Body Theory in Section II is a great place to start.

Alternatively, if you still can't take your own Light Body seriously by the end of this chapter, then hopefully I will have planted a

---

[12] Religion scholar Jeffrey Kripal calls this inner acceptance of greater human potential "making the flip." See Kripal, Jeffrey. (2019) *The Flip: Epiphanies of Mind and the Future of Knowledge*. Belleview Literary Press.

seed in your knowing, and it will sprout when the time is right. Come back later and the rest of the book will make more sense.

THE TEST

On the morning of September 11, 2001, I was at the Memphis airport, anticipating flying home to Denver. I arrived at my gate and settled into a seat, unpacking a few things to bide the time while I waited for boarding.

Then, I heard a whisper in my head (or I just knew in my insides) "Don't sit here. Everyone is going to be looking at me because there's a TV right above my head." When I heard/thought/knew this, no one was looking at me or watching the TV. It was broadcasting a morning SkyTV show featuring innocuous public-interest stories.

Nevertheless, I packed up my things, and I moved across the aisle to a seat that positioned me to face the TV. Fifteen minutes later, the broadcast was interrupted by President Bush announcing that planes had hit the Twin Towers and all aircraft were grounded. Everyone in my vicinity stopped what they were doing and looked in the direction of my former seat to watch the TV. I was glad I had moved.

This story from my life is an example of an instance that passes what I call *The Test*. I performed a behavior based on information I could not have obtained through my "normal" perceptual systems.

The Test:
Have you ever performed a behavior based on information you could not have obtained through "normal" perceptual systems?

If your answer is Yes, then you must adopt a world view that says what you did is possible.

A Yes answer is personal, so passing The Test is going to look different for everybody. Search your memory. When a Yes experience happened, you were probably surprised by your action, but you didn't think about it too much. It may even seem normal to you. Some people do it all the time without noticing.

If you're not sure an experience qualifies, think about the *behavior* you did and if you were likely to do that behavior without that particular information. Think about the *information* you used and where it could and could not have come from. If you *know* that you responded appropriately based on information that you *knew*, it proves to yourself that you didn't just imagine the information. Don't doubt your capabilities.

If you're saying to yourself, "This is just an experiment with an n of 1, so it doesn't have enough statistical power to prove anything," you'd be correct. However, if you have had even one experience that qualifies as a Yes, then there is no third-party belief system about reality that can override what you *know*. You don't have to justify yourself with data to any group or authority figure.

If no one has encouraged you before now to trust your intuitive experiences, you may be shocked to realize that you've been selling yourself short. It might be hard to accept that your understanding of reality needs to change in a significant way.

You will surprise yourself when you make this change, but I assure you that you are in good company. I have been coaching scientists and academics to accept their Light Bodies as real since my pandemic project obliged me to come "out of the closet" as someone who's comfortable with expanded consciousness. I meet people in all professions who are relieved to have their experiences validated. Critics of materialism are everywhere because it's not an accurate reflection of the human experience. It's an outdated paradigm that looks like Swiss cheese there are so many holes.

If, however, you've searched your memory, and your answer to The Test is "No," you can *manifest* having a Yes experience.

Decide right now that you want to have an experience that passes The Test. Say out loud, "I want to have an experience that incontrovertibly proves to me that I use information I could not have perceived through my normal senses."

I assure you that if you decide to learn more about your own capabilities, you will learn that you have more capabilities than you thought.

For real. This is not a joke. This is your life. You were born into this body to use your life. You sleep and wake and move around in consciousness all the time, and there was a time before you were born and a time after you will die.

REMOTE VIEWING

I'm amazed by my personal exploration of consciousness. I've been over-thinking things by myself for a long time, and now I want to have conversations. It's a challenge for me to figure out where to begin so I don't scare people away with lunatic vibes.

I've found one topic, Remote Viewing, that's a good first baby step for people starting on this journey with me. There is a lot of credible research on Remote Viewing, and you can easily try it yourself. When people learn more about Remote Viewing, they quickly understand why I'm excited about all this.

Please spend some time with this chapter. Look up the first-hand evidence and try Remote Viewing for yourself. It will make it easier to see why we need the theories in Sections II and III. It will help you understand the significance of Section IV, which includes my worry that our ignorance of the Light Body could be weaponized against us.

WHAT IS REMOTE VIEWING?

If you've never heard of Remote Viewing, you're in for a treat. If you've heard of it but you thought it was merely the butt of a joke, you're in for a treat. In this section I will briefly cover Remote Viewing and explain what's important and what's not important about it.

What's important is that Remote Viewing proves the existence of the Light Body. For more than 50 years, Remote Viewing experiments conducted by a variety of respectable researchers have found significant, reproducible effects that provide proof for the Stephens Gain Theorem. It proves that human anatomy has Non-Newtonian adaptations.

However (and this is a big however), it's easy to dismiss Remote Viewing entirely because the spying part seems so silly. Let's take a look.

In the latter part of the 20th century, the United States government secretly developed a program to use "paranormal," "extrasensory perception," "precognition," "telepathy," and "clairvoyant" phenomena for military gain. (Note - I consider much of the vocabulary used in their work to be outdated and loaded with baggage, so I put those words inside quotation marks to denote that I avoid language like this in my own work.)

The easiest way to learn about the US Government's Remote Viewing program is by watching the 2019 documentary film *Third Eye Spies*. It was produced by Russell Targ, one of the original researchers in the field.

To learn how to do Remote Viewing, I recommend the 1991 book *Everybody's Guide to Natural ESP*. It was written by Ingo Swann, one of the program's psychic spies.[13]

For further research, you can read the first-hand documents that were declassified in 2002. The CIA's website has a lot of free information, so I'll get you started by recommending three documents you can find easily by searching for the titles.[14]

—Mumford, Rose, & Goslin (1995). *An Evaluation of Remote Viewing: Research and Applications.* The American Institutes for Research.   CIA-RDP96-00791R000200180006-4.pdf

—Hubbard & Langford (1986). *A Suggested Remote Viewing Training Procedure.* SRI International.
CIA-RDP96-00789R002200070001-0.pdf

—Targ & Puthoff (1974). *Remote Viewing of Natural Targets.*
CIA-RDP96-00787R000500410001-3.pdf

The 1995 document is a review of the entire program that the government hired outside scientists[15] to perform. I'll summarize its important points with three quotes from their conclusions.

1 -They suspected that Remote Viewing is a latent human ability.

> "If certain people (or all people to a greater or lesser extent, as has been proposed by some investigators)

---

[13] Or visit the International Remote Viewing Association at irva.org
[14] The TriforiumTribune.com links page has links to these documents.
[15] Jessica Utts & Raymond Hyman, professors of Statistics & Psychology

possess the ability to see and describe target locations they have not visited, this ability might prove of great value to the intelligence community."

2 - The research concluded that yes, it is a latent human ability, but they did not understand the phenomena.

"A statistically significant effect has been observed in the recent laboratory experiments of remote viewing. ... No compelling explanation has been provided for the observed effects."

3 - It was not useful for government spying, so the program was discontinued.

"Remote viewings have never provided an adequate basis for "actionable" intelligence operations — that is, information sufficiently valuable or compelling enough so that action was taken as a result."

INTERPRETING REMOTE VIEWING

I feel like the kid calling out the emperor's nudity when I tell mainstream scientists that the implications of Remote Viewing are massive, so they should wake up and see it. Based on the Remote Viewing research and the ease at which people can be trained to do it, anyone who trusts science should be gobsmacked with amazement to know that humans can perceive non-local information. Anyone who studies any human phenomena should accommodate that fact into everything they do.

In addition to authoring the 1974 document about their initial research, Russell Targ and Harold Puthoff published their results (including astoundingly accurate drawings) in the prestigious journal *Nature*[16] in 1974. Two of their conclusions are quoted here.

> "A channel exists whereby information about a remote location can be obtained by means of an as yet unidentified perceptual modality."

> "It may be that remote perceptual ability is widely distributed in the general population, but because the perception is generally below an individual's level of awareness, it is repressed or not noticed. For example, two of our subjects (H.H. and P.P) had not considered themselves to have unusual perceptual ability before their participation in these experiments."

So why doesn't anyone care?

The evidence for Remote Viewing has had no impact because it is stuck in the framework of military intelligence gathering. When Remote Viewing was developed, academia had not yet adopted the use of evolutionary approaches to understand the human mind. The people who did Remote Viewing research did not apply insights from biological evolution to unravel the subtleties of the phenomena they documented. I suspect that many of them were also emotionally depleted by the controversy. It's too hard to argue with skeptics, so many of them gave up in frustration, yet they were still obliged to secrecy. Eventually they were mocked by Hollywood with a satirical movie that convinced the public that they failed (*Men Who Stare at Goats*, 2009).

Until recently, I ignored Remote Viewing too because the spying stuff seems absurd. From a biological standpoint, there's no

---

[16] Targ R and Puthoff H. Information transmission under conditions of sensory shielding. *Nature* 251, 602–607 (1974).

reason to think that our species would have undergone natural selection for non-local spying to evolve.[17]

If we use a different approach, however, Remote Viewing can be analyzed as a demonstration of a Non-Newtonian species trait. Evolution by natural selection provides the theoretical foundation to explore it further. We can use an Adaptationist Perspective to unravel the subtleties of the phenomena for evolutionarily relevant things. That's what Light Body Theory provides in Sections II and III.

It is also notable that the government-funded program was ostensibly canceled because it got a "No" answer for The Test. In the 1995 review, it was reported that the military had never performed a behavior based on information that was obtained by Remote Viewing. Former President Jimmy Carter, however, reported otherwise in his 2016 memoir:

> "One morning I had a report from the CIA that a small twin-engine plane had gone down somewhere in Zaire, and that it contained some important secret documents. We were searching for the crash site using satellite photography and some other surreptitious high-altitude overflights, but with no success. With some hesitancy, a CIA agent in California recommended the services of a clairvoyant woman who was then consulted. She wrote down a latitude and longitude, which proved to be accurate, and several days later I was shown a photograph of the plane, totally destroyed and in a remote area."[18]

---

[17] Or is there a reason? Will evolutionary psychologists take my bait?
[18] Carter, Jimmy (2016) *A Full Life: Reflections at Ninety*. Simon & Schuster.

There is further evidence that the US Military should give a "Yes" answer for The Test. It was reported in three autobiographical memoirs that in 1987, the Air National Guard used information from a psychic to find yet another crashed airplane.[19]

Remote Viewing continues to be relevant today. Over the course of two decades, hundreds of people worked on the program, and many of them have written books about it since it was declassified. There are still traditional Psychology academics researching it.[20] In addition, there are regular people teaching themselves to do it. These people usually just want to predict the stock market or find lost items, but they maintain online public databases that you can use to try it out. That's what we're going to do next.

TRY REMOTE VIEWING

Remote Viewing is not a natural or normal thing for anyone to do, but I want you to try it now because a percentage of readers will discover that you are already surprisingly good at it.

I hope you found the document "A Suggested Remote Viewing Training Procedure". If you skim it, you'll see that they used a lot of jargon and protocols to make it military style. You don't need any of that to try it for yourself.

---

[19] The crashed plane was piloted by Dean Paul Martin, the entertainer Dean Martin's son. See these three memoirs:

Margolis, Char. (1999) *Questions from Earth, Answers from Heaven: a psychic intuitive's discussion of life, death, and what awaits us beyond.* St. Martin's Press.

Martin, Deana. (2005) *Memories are Made of This: Dean Martin through his Daughter's Eyes.* Crown Publishing.

Martin, Ricci and Smith, Christopher (2004) *That's Amore: A Son Remembers Dean Martin.* Taylor Trade Publishing.

[20] Schooler J, Baumgart S, Franklin M. (2018) Entertaining Without Endorsing: The Case for the Scientific Investigation of Anomalous Cognition. *Psychology of Consciousness.* Vol 5: 63-77.

To practice Remote Viewing, you'll need:

- A piece of paper
- A writing utensil
- An online dataset of remote viewing targets.[21]

You'll need a quiet time and space where you won't be bothered, and you'll need enthusiasm for the possibility that you might learn something new about yourself.

These are my general directions. Read through the directions entirely before you begin.

---

21 Links to a Target Pool at TriforiumTribune.com links page.

Lessons In Knowing

1 - Sit at a computer and **find a Target Pool** on the internet.

2 - **Get a Label (usually a number or an alphanumeric code) that assigns you to a New Target.** Depending on the database, you may have to click on a button, a link, or a bullseye to get assigned a new Label (or you might just need to choose one from a list of Labels). Each Label is associated with a particular Target that is a real place somewhere on the Earth. (Some data sets may also give you neutral information they call "Frontloading." That's just military jargon, don't worry about it.)

3 - When you see the Label, **use your imagination to "visit" the Target location.** Allow yourself to visualize that space. What do you see? What do you hear? What do you notice about the Target location? What comes to mind? Images, shapes, textures, colors, objects, words, sounds, ideas... ? Do whatever you do best to focus on your imagination. If you are a reader, then "read," if you're a listener, then "listen," if you're a daydreamer, then "daydream."

4 - **Write or Draw Three Observations on paper.** Describe as much as you get, even the extra words that don't seem meaningful. If you draw a shape, describe that shape with words. It's important that you actually put your observations in writing so you don't question yourself later.

5 - After you write down three observations, **click the "Feedback" button to reveal a photo of the Target.**

6 - **Rate your observations.** It's a "Hit" if one or more observations describe what's in the photo.

In a typical Remote Viewing practice session, a viewer "Views" multiple Targets, one after another. I suggest viewing five targets in a row, then taking a break.

There is a pattern that you should know about. It's common for people to get Hits right away, then they freak out and get Misses on the following attempts. After a while, they recover and get Hits again. This pattern has been well documented throughout the history of psi experimentation, and you will probably experience it too. It's called a "decline effect," or a "rubber band pattern."[22]

Keep in mind that you're practicing a new skill, using "muscles" you may not have exercised since you were a kid. You will learn more about yourself if you keep going and you experiment. Try doing it multiple days in a row. Try doing it at different times of day. Try doing it while you drink a cup of coffee or after you exercise. Try doing it when you're sleepy.

AFTER YOU REMOTE VIEW

Now that you've tried Remote Viewing, I hope you can see that it is a way for you to take The Test. It's not naturalistic, but if you got a Hit, then writing the observation was the behavior you did based on information you acquired in a Non-Newtonian way. It doesn't matter that you don't know how you did it or that people probably do it in different ways. It's a skill, something you can practice to improve.

I'll remind you that if you can now say "Yes," I passed The Test, then it's time to outgrow strict materialism. If you got just one Hit that was surprisingly, maybe even shockingly, specific, then it's not crazy to see that it wasn't just a statistical anomaly. If that makes you feel lost and confused, then you're in good company. I hope Section I of this book has helped you realize you live in a bigger world than you thought you did. Light Body Theory in

---

[22] Herb Mertz described it in agonizing detail in his memoir about creating products with PEAR random event generators.
 Mertz, Herb (2020) *The Selection Effect: How Consciousness Shapes Reality*. Penn Wolcott Press

Section II will give you a new orientation to head in the right direction.

If you're intrigued and you want to learn more about your own capabilities to access information in a Non-Newtonian way, there is another popular training method I suggest you try. There are online datasets for people to practice The Silva Method[23] of energy healing. Silva casework is like Remote Viewing about people instead of locations, so you already know how to do it, and you can try your hand (ha ha) at healing too. Search "Silva Method Casework Practice" to find these datasets and learn more. (Links on the TriforiumTribune.com links page.)

---

[23] Silva, Jose. (1989) You The Healer: The World Famous Silva Mind Control Method to Heal Yourself and Others. HJ Kramer

CHAPTER FOUR

No Time For Skeptics

Now that you've made it to the end of this section, I hope you're thinking differently about your body and what it can do. It takes bravery to change your self-identity, so I encourage you to relax and take your time.

As a reward for your efforts, take a YouTube break and watch Apollo astronaut Edgar Mitchell answer "What is Consciousness?" In less than 4 minutes, he explains how entanglement and non-locality are experienced by humans, even though it's taboo to talk about it. [24]

Regarding the taboo, I suspect that it was the work of one very high-profile scientist that steered most people away from consciousness research involving Non-Newtonian phenomena. Nobel Prize winner Francis Crick had rock-star status for discovering the DNA double helix when, at the end of his career, he promoted a materialist view that consciousness spontaneously

---

[24] Mitchell, Edgar (2016) *Tell Me a Story: Edgar Mitchell "What is Consciousness"* Kennedy Space Center Visitor Complex on YouTube. (Link on TriforiumTribune.com links page)

arises from neural activity in the brain.[25] His views became dogma in the field of Psychology. They created inertia for Biologists and Doctors of Medicine to limit their imaginations to Classical Physics, even though the field of Physics had moved on.

But what if you're not ready to accept the possibility of Non-Newtonian human anatomy? People are all different, so I know some readers will still be skeptical.

In some academic circles it's an expected tradition to pander to skeptics, so I'll explain why I won't do that. Everyone has a Light Body and is using their Light Body all the time, whether they believe it or not. I'll indulge in a wizarding metaphor to say that some skeptics are people who perform black magic to shut other people down.[26] If you feel your Light Body as I do, sometimes interacting with a skeptic can feel like a tight squeezing strangulation. It's a bad physical feeling that takes effort to resist and recover from. In our culture, we give skeptics too much influence because we don't have an "emic" representation of the Light Body. (I'll explain what that means in Part II.)

There is research that demonstrates that skeptics are not energetically benign. They, like everyone else, see their beliefs reflected back to them. For this experiment, a skeptic and a gnostic (someone who knows psi phenomena to be true) performed the same experimental protocol in the same lab with the same subject pool. Then they compared results.

According to the protocol, the experimenter looked at participants intermittently through a closed-circuit television system, and they analyzed biometric data (skin resistance) to test if the participants could detect their unseen gaze.

---

[25] Crick, Francis and Christoff Koch (1990) Towards a Neurobiological theory of Consciousness. Seminars in the Neurosciences, Vol 2: 263-275.
[26] I'll explain this in Part III as Witnessing.

For the gnostic experimenter, the data showed a significant effect ($p < .05$).

For the skeptic experimenter, the data did NOT show a significant effect ($p > .05$). [27]

The implications of experimenter effects like this are widespread and profound.

Skepticism is not the same as scientific discernment.

The replication crisis in psychology will not be solved without understanding the Light Body and accommodating its effects into research protocols.

Thankfully, more and more people are stepping into a new paradigm that better reflects the human experience.

---

[27] Wiseman R & Schlitz M. (1997) Experimenter Effects and the Remote Detection of Staring. *Journal of Parapsychology*, 61(3) 197-208.

Part Two
LIGHT BODY THEORY

E. Stephens Gain

CHAPTER FIVE

Light Body Theory

We use our subtle energy systems in everything we do and everywhere we go, including public spaces. If we want to be open about it, then we need a theoretical framework that everyone can agree on. Understanding our Light Bodies to be a Human Universal offers such a framework.

Human Universals is a concept put forward by anthropologist Donald Brown in his 1991 book of the same name. With this approach, it's understood that the human species isn't just defined by our biological anatomy, we also have cognitive "anatomy" that can be revealed by looking at the traits common to all human cultures.

The theory behind Human Universals transforms our understanding of non-physical human phenomena into legitimate traits that can be understood through the lens of science. In Brown's words, Human Universals "consist of those features of culture, society, language, behavior, and mind that, so far as the record has been examined, are found among all peoples known to ethnography and history."[28] Understanding a trait to be a Human

---

[28] Brown, Donald. 2004. Human universals, human nature & human culture. *Daedalus* 133 (4): 47-54. https://doi.org/10.1162/0011526042365645

Universal invites it to be researched through scientific observation and hypothesis testing based on the theoretical principles of evolutionary biology and evolutionary psychology.

In this chapter, I propose that the Light Body is indeed such a Human Universal. I'll describe what I mean by Light Body, and I'll explain my evidence for this.

These are my theories based on my own exploration of consciousness and my understanding of evolutionary biology and evolutionary psychology. It is also based on my acceptance of modern theoretical physics.

DEFINING THE LIGHT BODY

Humans are born, we live in a body for a lifetime, and then we die. We are awake, we go to sleep, we dream, and we wake up. We perceive through our bodies, we move our bodies, we communicate with our bodies, we use our bodies to make new bodies.

Every living human is consciousness "incarnated" into a body, and incarnation involves a system for the interface of consciousness and matter. There are real limitations on how well we can understand this system. However, we can know and understand more about it than is commonly accepted. We benefit from not ignoring this amazing system that we all experience.

The "Light Body" is the substance of all natural incarnation material simplified into a name that's easy to understand. It will bring society great comfort to use this idea on a practical level. Individuals, groups, and institutions alike will obtain more creative fulfillment if we acknowledge what we can do with our Light Bodies.

The idea of the Light Body is not new. It has been understood throughout the millennia because it is a basic truth of human existence.

Our modern culture, however, is a historical product of religious violence in Europe. Our ancestors traversed through hardships where they were obligated to shut down their awareness of the Light Body to prevent further violence and upheaval in our societies. It was appropriate for them to do that, and it had the intended effect of springing our culture toward a radically different pathway than where we were originally headed. Nothing was wrong with what we did to ourselves.

Today, however, we want to understand how to use our latent capacities. This is a powerful drive in everyone living in cultures descended from the Roman Empire. You can see it in the popularity of superheroes and wizards in movies and fantasies. You can see it in the popularity of non-European philosophies and knowledge traditions like Yoga and Buddhism. You can see it in the growing acceptance of Alternative Medicine. We are revealing to ourselves healthy ways to bring forth these capacities again.

It is on us to do it right this time. With the theory of the Light Body as a Human Universal, we can progress toward where we have never been. Acceptance of the Light Body will launch us into a new paradigm of human knowledge.

LIGHT BODY IS HUMAN ANATOMY

The Light Body is just like your regular body, except it's made out of a different energetic substance that is not yet currently understood. It was subject to the same evolutionary processes as your physical body. It has accrued functional complexity in the same way, and its adaptive design can be teased apart in much the same way as the physical body.

The Light Body is different, however, because it exists in physical dimensions that are outside the design parameters of our social communication systems. There is an incompatibility between our Light Bodies and some of our other intelligence systems that evolved to be specific to "Newtonian" physics principles. Everyone uses both bodies - one made out of matter and one made of non-matter (our cells probably don't distinguish between the two); but our social intelligence evolved to enable us to talk about one, not the other.

For that reason, we are left with mysteries of perception and knowing, and different cultures have invented their own specific ways to interpret those mysteries.

That's what I'm doing now with this book. By defining the Light Body, I'm inventing a new cultural way to interpret those mysteries. I'm developing it with parameters to maintain its acceptability within our modern societal structures. This is not a religious idea. It adheres to the principles of science.

Take a moment now and think about YOUR Light Body. (I'm pointing at you!) Your Light Body is your anatomy to use and live through in your lifetime. It's beyond time, and it's outside of the spacial restrictions of three-dimensional matter. I encourage you to try to see how you've been taught to deny its existence. I encourage you to decide something new.

WHY WE NEED THIS THEORY

In US History class, do you remember learning that the United States attracted early settlers because of William Penn's promise of religious freedom? Our country was founded by people seeking refuge from religious violence that had plagued Europe for thousands of years. Thankfully, valuing religious freedom is built into our society.

However, these freedoms came with a detrimental side-effect. The denial of the anatomical truth of our subtle-energy intelligence is also built into our society. This denial dominates our culture to the extent that teaching subtle-energy intelligence has even been whitewashed out of the majority of modern American religious practice. (Religion scholars call this cessationism.)

As a result, individuals who want to actuate their potential to use subtle-energy intelligence will need to overcome many fears both privately and publicly. People developing Light Body skills may worry that they are doing something wrong, unnatural, religious, anti-religious, dangerous, or occult. All those fears have been internalized into our society because of our violent history of religious persecution, and we need a way out.

Having a culturally endorsed Light Body Theory is necessary to give us a fresh start and re-claim more of our human potential.

CHAPTER SIX

Using Human Universals Theory

As strange as it might sound, the human Light Body is real, and it's invisible. How can we understand it?

In his 2004 article entitled *Human universals, human nature & human culture,*[29] anthropologist Donald E. Brown succinctly explains how the theory of Human Universals enables us to study invisible cultural phenomena as adaptive mechanisms shaped by evolution. This approach is particularly suited to understanding the Light Body because it is invisible too, and it must necessarily have evolved through natural selection.

Natural selection is a "blind" process that builds complexity with everything available to the system at the time of the selection. There is no reason to think that Non-Newtonian physics properties would have been excluded at any moment of our evolutionary development. Therefore, The Light Body must have contributed to our evolutionary history with the same significance as our visible, three-dimensional, physical anatomy.

---

[29] Brown, Donald. (2004) Human universals, human nature & human culture. *Daedalus* Fall 2004: 47-54.
https://doi.org/10.1162/0011526042365645

Applying Brown's Human Universals theory to understand the Light Body illuminates a variety of surprising revelations. Go get a copy of Brown's 2004 article now so you can follow along as I outline what this means. (See TriforiumTribune.com links page.)

EMIC AND ETIC

On the first and second pages, Brown explains the significance of classifying anthropological features as being either "emic" or "etic."

> "These words (derived from the linguistic terms "phonemic" and "phonetic') distinguish features that are overtly or consciously represented in a people's own cultural conceptions from features that are present but not a part of the overt or conscious local cultural conceptions."

The emic/etic demarcation is particularly informative when applied to Light Body phenomena. *Etically*, every human has a Light Body. The Stephens Gain Theorem proves this as an anatomical fact, so the Light Body is an *etic* universal. *Emically*, however, there is variance in the cultural representation of the Light Body (e.g. Indian doshas and chakras or Chinese meridians). Some cultures may not have a cultural representation of the Light Body at all. The Light Body is not an *emic* universal.

Mainstream materialist culture in the United States is an obvious example of a culture that does NOT yet have an *emic* representation of the Light Body. Light Body Theory is an attempt to give mainstream United States culture an *emic* representation.

SUBTLE ENERGY IS HERE TO STAY

European-descended, "Western" society pretends to be blind to the Light Body (and we do our best to ignore it), but we still feel it. In the United States today, "mindfulness" has become normalized, but many who try it want it to go deeper. "Subtle energy" addresses deeper feelings, but that is a confusing term for many people. Most people understand subtle energy to be the same thing as Chi, kundalini, and prana, whose foreign origins evoke respect as real, unlike Mesmer's "animal magnetism" which is still derided as fake.

We are a bit mixed-up because of the *emic* we're missing.

Scientists and academics have avoided it but the public wants it, so there are many individuals filling the vacuum. Practical advice on esoteric matters is plentiful on the internet from channelers, influencers, and alternative medicine gurus. This cultural outpouring is welcomed and craved by the public, and in many ways it truly helps people. However, those offering marketplace wisdom are obliged to structure their offerings to support their livelihoods. This leads to an abundance of gurus inventing new proprietary vocabularies anchored around charismatic figureheads.

What's the alternative?

Light Body Theory is the simplest foundation of agreement for scientists and academics to construct a new paradigm of knowledge.

So how do we study the Light Body? What questions should we be asking? That's what the next chapter is about.

CHAPTER SEVEN
Mental Mechanisms & Variability

The most ingenious part of Don Brown's seminal paper is an extended discussion of "universals of mind," starting at the end of page 50. It is this content that is most pertinent for our current use. It instructs us how to understand the Light Body with an adaptationist perspective based on principles of evolution by natural selection.

Brown was an anthropologist versed in the ways of analyzing culture, so the main aspect he directs us to think about is *variability*. We need to know how a constant universal is manifested with the variability seen among human individuals and between cultures. Variability is a prediction of evolutionary theory that can be revealed by the science of evolutionary psychology.[30] He provides five distinct discussions about underlying causes of the variability we see.

Below, I will apply the ideas in each of his five discussions to my understanding of the Light Body. Doing so reveals surprising potential for the significance of the Light Body in human affairs.

---

[30] Cosmides, Leda and John Tooby (1987) From Evolution to Behavior: Evolutionary Psychology as the Missing Link. in Dupre, John (Ed), *The Latest on the Best: Essays on Evolution and Optimality*, MIT Press. Ch 13.

First, Brown emphasizes the role of evolution in creating numerous mechanisms, each with a particular adaptive function. "The set of mental mechanisms that comprise the human mind, and that are thus fundamental to human nature, were designed by natural selection to solve particular problems that were recurrent in our evolutionary past and that are presumably finite in number."

Human Universals provides a theoretical foundation to understand the Light Body as a subtle-energy intelligence system inextricably enmeshed with the mental mechanisms Brown describes. Originating in parallel with the evolution of our physical anatomy, the Light Body is a complex web of mental and bodily mechanisms that evolved due to their capacity to affect evolutionarily adaptive behaviors.

Evolutionary selection pressures acted with Newtonian and Non-Newtonian properties simultaneously. Therefore, the Light Body is embedded in all functions of our physical body and mental capabilities. *Everything we know about the human body - homeostasis, reproduction, metabolism, respiration, memory, language, learning, birth, death - must necessarily have a subtle-energy component operating in tandem with our physical body.* This means that our physical organs have a companion Light Body organ. We have physical lungs and Light Body lungs, a physical brain and a Light Body brain, physical hands and Light Body hands, physical mitochondria and Light Body mitochondria.

To make sense of variability, Brown instructs us to make a distinction between the adaptive function versus the potential side-effects of an evolved universal trait. In this regard, I consider Remote Viewing to be an example of a side-effect of an evolved Light Body trait. As I mentioned earlier, there's no reason to think that our species would have undergone selection pressures specifically for non-local spying to evolve, but this ability must have provided evolutionarily significant benefits to those who could do it. Therefore, research on Remote Viewing should try to uncover the adaptive function of the capabilities used in Remote Viewing. Using an adaptationist perspective could have provided direction for the military intelligence professionals who were stymied by puzzles that seemed intractable.

Second, Brown explains that many mental mechanisms are not hyper-specific, but they are directed toward big-picture survival goals like food-acquisition and reproduction. Likewise, the functions of the Light Body should be evaluated as potential contributors to the mental mechanisms for fulfilling those goals. For example, I would suggest that our need to be safe and to detect danger are broad mental-mechanism goals that contain a significant Light Body component. Phrases like "basking in a golden glow" and "shivers up my spine" give clues about the Light Body perceptual experience of these mechanisms.

Third, Brown explains that some mental mechanisms are "variable by design." They require *calibration* from experience with the environment. He gives beauty standards as an example. When I apply this idea to what I know about the Light Body, I discover a host of significant and surprising possibilities regarding human development.

I propose that Light Bodies have some sort of reproductive process that parallels the life history of the physical body, e.g. conception, gestation, birth, childhood, adulthood, and death. Personal accounts (e.g. near-death experiences) and channeled literature are our only sources of insight about this process.

Similarly, I propose there is variability among Light Bodies according to yet unknown parameters. Just as some people are tall and some people short, some people have bigger Light Bodies than others. Light Bodies have features that can differ between individuals and between groups. Some cultures have *emic* representations of this variability (e.g. chakras, astrology, Kabbalah, the Human Design System).

Next, I propose that there are certain aspects of Light Body functioning that are foundationally shaped during early childhood. This can be seen as a kind of language learning. As babies progress through developmental stages to learn the language of their family, they also learn how to "sing," "listen," "witness," and "know" with their Light Bodies according to the way their family members do. They learn to *move* their Light Bodies in the way their family members do. Because of this transmission, the "culture" of Light Body functioning would not remain static. The Light Body expressed by the adult would be experienced as the environmental baseline by the child. Through multiple generations, people could become very different from what they were before.

Along the same lines, I propose another idea that has surprising consequences to displace DNA's supremacy as the only place where adaptational complexity can evolve. During the 9 months of gestation, the mother's Light Body overlaps with the Light Body of the developing fetus. This allows for imprinting of the fetal Light Body due to prolonged and predictable exposure to the mother's Light Body. The mother's Light Body would necessarily have been influenced by her life experiences, and this could be passed on to her offspring. Therefore, Light Body imprinting could be a yet undiscovered pathway for the inheritance of acquired traits, *aka* Lamarckian Evolution. (It's also possible that Light Body imprinting from the father could occur, but through a different pathway.) This could inform the relatively new field of epigenetics that investigates how trauma-informed patterns of genetic expression are inherited by children (and baby rats) whose parents had PTSD.[31]

---

[31] Yehuda, Rachel. (2022) Trauma in the Family Tree. *Scientific American Magazine* 327(1) 50. doi: 10.1038/scientificamerican0722-50

In a surprising twist of insight, we should also remember that Non-Newtonian properties happen on a radically different scale than we are accustomed to using. It's possible that there could be unusual Non-Newtonian imprinting influences on the Light Body, such as the gravitational pull of large bodies of matter like planets and stars. (The ancient Greeks' music of the spheres!) At birth, the Light Body could be initialized to a snapshot of gravitational forces like the way the tare button sets a zero point on a scale. Astoundingly, this idea gives credence to astrology.

Fourth, Brown explains how our behavior arises from complex interactions of mechanisms, sometimes with conflicting goals. This describes the challenge that Evolutionary Psychologists face when they attempt to tease apart the relevant factors at play within any phenomenon. You would expect a subtle-energy intelligence system to be complicated.

Fifth, Brown explains how environmental variability is another reason we see significant variability between individuals and populations. Regarding the Light Body, exposure to different or unusual kinds of radiation could be an environmental influence. Examples are "space weather" from changes in the solar wind or the "vortexes" of subtle energy that are felt in some geographic locations by people sensitive to them (e.g. Sedona, AZ).

When looking at Light Body Intelligence mechanisms, you also must keep in mind that there can be environmental mis-matches that disrupt their adaptive functioning. Evolutionary theory explains that there can be aspects of modern environments that are mis-matched from the environments in which the adaptation evolved (the Environment of Evolutionary Adaptedness, aka the

---

(31 cont.) Mulligan CJ et al. (2025) Epigenetic signatures of intergenerational exposure to violence in three generations of Syrian refugees. *Scientific Reports* (15)5945.

EEA.[32]). Therefore, we might see strange or novel outcomes that could be considered non-adaptive.

In addition, the cultural environment could play a significant role in Light Body expression. You could expect there to be group-defining aspects such as subtle-energy structures, habits, or sensitivity thresholds that distinguish one group from another. Anthropologists use the term ethnoepistemology to refer to the ways a particular understanding of embodiment influences a culture.[33] It's my perspective that differences in ethnoepistemology between cultures arise because of different norms for Light Body expression.

Differences in aspects of the environment that influence Light Bodies could result in very different experiences of "reality" and "stream of consciousness" between cultures. Understanding how this is possible could explain seemingly unresolvable conflicts between cultures. If you know that the underlying source of the conflict is a difference in Light Body Intelligence systems, you have a new perspective from which to seek resolution.

I can suggest a few cultural differences along this vein. For example, the prevalence of Hindu gods as real non-bodied entities does not parse in the United States' Christian-derived *emic* Light Body expression, so we "believe" that Hindu gods are merely imaginary. Similarly, the Christian Bible documents stories about people who experienced reality in a vastly different way than is possible for us to experience today. The Light Body Intelligence system structures from a thousand years ago have evolved into a

---

[32] The EEA is an important concept. Re-read that sentence if you need to. When you read the term EEA, imagine hunter-gatherer tribes living in the Pleistocene, eating a Paleo diet.

[33] Locke, Ralph G. & Kelly, Edward F. (1985) A Preliminary Model for the Cross-cultural Analysis of Altered States of Consciousness. *Ethos* 13(1): 3-55.

new "operating system" that is incompatible with the previous operating system in significant ways.

WHAT'S NEXT?

"Innate human universals continuously and pervasively structure human culture."
~ Donald Brown

Brown suggests that we "back-engineer" any cultural phenomena we observe by seeing it as a manifestation of universal truths about human nature.

I propose that we back-engineer the list of Human Universals to understand more about the Light Body. That's the subject of the next chapter.

CHAPTER EIGHT

Evidence for the Light Body

In this section, I will outline the evidence for the Light Body. This is not intended to be an exhaustive list, and I'm not going to spend time going into detail here. If your curiosity is piqued to do your own research, this outline will direct you where to look for further information.

EVIDENCE FROM THE LIST OF HUMAN UNIVERSALS

In 1991, Don Brown and friends' list of Human Universals sparked much discussion among academics, and an updated "official list" was published as an appendix of Steven Pinker's 2002 book, *The Blank Slate*. There is ongoing discussion, and it's understood that there are many more traits yet to be recognized as a Human Universal. There is no official system in place to maintain this list.

The following is a subset of traits from this list that I selected because I consider them to be evidence that the Light Body is a Human Universal. It's my perspective that the invisible Light Body is a relevant underlying anatomy that is expressed through these observable traits.

Divination
Belief in supernatural/religion
Beliefs about disease
Dreams
Dream interpretation
Emotions
Empathy
Gestures
Healing the sick (or attempting to)
Language not a simple reflection of reality
Magic
Magic to increase life
Magic to sustain life
Magic to win love
Melody
Memory
Metaphor
Mood or consciousness-altering techniques or substances
Music
Music related in part to religious activity
Music seen as art
Music - 10 variations to describe how humans use music
Normal distinguished from abnormal states
Private inner life
Rhythm
Self - distinguished from other
Self as neither wholly passive nor wholly autonomous
Senses unified
Symbolism
Symbolic speech
True & false distinguished
Weather control (attempts to)
Worldview
Critical learning periods
Imagery
Intention

Mentalese
Self-image
Synesthetic metaphors

It should be noted that Materialism and Time are also on the Human Universals List. I would argue that the cognitive structures underlying these two traits are what limit our awareness of the Light Body. The Light Body, by definition, is Non-Newtonian, so it exists outside of space and time.

EVIDENCE FROM CULTURAL AND RELIGIOUS COSMOLOGY

> "To be evangelical about anything means you only learned once."
>
> ~ E. Stephens Gain

I am someone who loves to step in and out of different worlds and different philosophical systems. Born and raised in the midwestern United States, educated on the East Coast, and living in California (and briefly in Boulder, CO) has given me ample opportunity to study and explore a variety of different religions, wisdom traditions, and new age practices.

I look for the truth in philosophical systems, and I always see the truth of the Light Body arising from our common anatomy. However, every system also has political baggage manifested as distortions of the truth. I keep an evolutionary perspective in mind, remembering that ancestral people would have been exposed only to the wisdom traditions of their local tribes. Wisdom traditions reflect the character of a particular culture.

If you immerse yourself in a particular wisdom tradition, you are likely to find directions for using the Light Body. When you find it, it may feel like discovering the One Truth because you're getting validation of your lived experience for the first time. If you

Evidence for the Light Body

keep exploring new worlds, however, you'll discover there are many truths. According to Light Body Theory, you've discovered one set of directions for using the Light Body, one particular batch of metaphors to make the invisible comprehensible to our intelligence systems. (That's called "Earthization." I'll discuss it later.)

This aspect of Light Body Theory is evidenced by the variety of religions and cultural cosmologies worldwide. If you look for it, you will find practical methodology for using the Light Body in all cultures throughout history. Here is my (apologetically incomplete) list of examples:

- Ka - the etheric body in Egyptian cosmology
- Chakra systems - from India
- Chi - of Chinese Medicine
- Qi Gong - from China
- The Holy Spirit - Christian traditions
- Reiki - from Japan
- Tree of Life - in Kabbalah Jewish mysticism
- Merkaba - in Kabbalah
- Christ Consciousness – Contemplative/Gnostic Christianity
- Subtle Energy Body - of the Rosicrucians
- Shamanic journeying - from Native Americans
- Ayurveda - from India
- The Bhagavad-Gita - from India
- Naam - of the Sikh tradition
- Mesmerism - 20th century Europe and United States
- Hypnotism - Europe and the United States

EVIDENCE FROM CHANNELED LITERATURE

In the past century, useful instruction on using the Light Body has been published by a variety of reputable, English-speaking Americans who channel non-physical entities. Here is my (apologetically incomplete) list.

   Jane Roberts (Seth)
   Paul Selig (The Guides/Melchizedek)
   Lee Harris (the Zs)
   Esther Hicks (Abraham)
   Alice A. Bailey (the Tibetan)
   Amorah Quan Yin (Pleiadians)
   Guy Ballard (St. Germain)
   Edgar Cayce
   Helen Cohn Schucman (A Course in Miracles)

If you're unfamiliar with channeled literature, see the Appendix entitled "Introduction to Channeled Literature."

EVIDENCE FROM SCIENTIFIC STUDIES

Ever since the dawn of science, people have been reinventing the wheel, discovering the Light Body over and over. These discoveries and experiments are published in books and papers, the official records of sanctioned scientific knowledge. These days, a simple internet search will unearth a large body of scientific evidence that cannot be explained by materialist thinking. Most modern scientists, however, are usually encouraged to ignore that evidence to conform to the mainstream professional communities that support their livelihoods.

As a result, scientific history is full of trends where people invent proprietary approaches with proprietary vocabulary to describe the phenomena of the Light Body. It often takes a charismatic figure to push for the truth, so there is often a personality and a cultural zeitgeist that shaped how the trend developed and why it lost favor. Below are a few examples of such trends.

In the 1700s, Anton Mesmer invented new healing methodologies based on phenomena he called "animal magnetism." Dominant medical establishments shut him down, but others picked up the reins. It was trendy in the late 1800s for people to experiment with Mesmerism. Following that trend, hypnotism became popular in the early 1900s, which led to the development of surgical anesthesia.

It was trendy in the 1970s for researchers to study telepathy, clairvoyance, remote viewing, and other phenomena described as ESP (Extra Sensory Perception, parodied in the movie *Ghostbusters*). This led to a proliferation of former engineers who performed serious research on consciousness in the 1980s and 90s, (e.g. William Tiller of Stanford, Robert Jahn and Brenda Dunne of the Princeton Engineering Anomalies Research lab (aka PEAR), Edgar Mitchell of NASA, William H. Kautz of SRI, and psychologist William Braud).[34] In their lifetimes, these researchers made huge progress on proving Light Body phenomena to be real. However, their financial support and public interest eventually waned before they could make progress on informing the public imagination.

The influence of these significant pioneers continues today with a new generation of researchers who picked up the reins. Thankfully, their numbers are growing every day, and it's hard

---

[34] Tiller, William (1997). Science and Human Transformation. Pavior.
Jahn, Robert and Brenda Dune (1987). Margins of Reality. Harcourt Brace Jovanovich
Mitchell, Edgar (1974). Psychic Exploration. Perigee.
Kautz, William (2005). Opening the Inner Eye. iUniverse.
Braud, William (2003). Distant Mental Influence. Hampton Roads.

for me to pick favorites to acknowledge in this book. Much of this research is applied to healing, and I would suggest the work of Richard Gordon, Lynn McTaggart, Eileen McKusick, and William Bengston[35] as easy to understand, not overly publicized, examples to refer interested readers. I'll also highlight the participants in the Global Consciousness Project and data/art scientists like P.e.a.c.e. !nc. who are performing ongoing research to apply PEAR's discoveries on mind-matter interactions.

Academia has been stuck in a purgatory of *proving* Light Body phenomena over and over. Adopting Light Body Theory will enable it to break out of that cycle and figure out what we can DO with our Light Bodies. What are we already doing with our Light Bodies? More importantly, we can see societal problems from a new perspective by asking, "Who is doing what to whom with their Light Bodies?"

All the historical research and documentation of human "anomalies" can be re-defined as the operation of our Light Bodies. Using evolutionary principles, we can understand the adaptive design of the Light Body to explain scientific evidence in the historical record.

RESISTANCE IN UNITED STATES CULTURE

How do we experience the Light Body in the United States?

Within each individual, the strongest evidence for the existence of the Light Body is not a statistic or a fact, it's our practical lived experience of reality. We're born with a Light Body, so everyone automatically uses it. We don't need permission from the

---

[35] Gordon, Richard (2006). *Quantum Touch*. North Atlantic Books.
McTaggart, Lynn (2008). *The Field* (updated edition). Harper Collins.
McKusick, Eileen (2021). *Electric Body, Electric Health*. St. Martins.
Bengston, William (2010). *The Energy Cure*. Sounds True.

authorities. We have imagination for it steeped within our cultural zeitgeist in our stories about wizards and superheroes. We differ in Light Body size, we differ in the ability to Feel our Light Bodies, we differ in how we use our Light Bodies, and only a minority fraction of our population has developed a healthy acceptance of it as real. (This book is attempting to change that.)

The Light Body is invisible to our "normal" vision; and, like most human traits, there is diversity in the ability to *Feel the Light Body*. Regarding the scope of human perception, our cultural norms oblige us to restrict public dialogue to the lowest common denominator. No one talks about perceiving the Light Body in public, so we effectively teach ourselves and our children to ignore the sensations of subtle energy. This makes sense to people who cannot feel their Light Bodies. People who can feel it, however, are deterred from paying attention to it and learning how to use it. On a practical level, people at one end of the spectrum - those who can NOT feel their Light Bodies - are allowed to gaslight everyone who can feel their Light Bodies.

For those who feel their Light Bodies, denying the influence of subtle energy does not reflect the reality of our lived experience. We crave validation and want to learn more, so we adopt practices from other cultures - Yoga, Chinese medicine, Kabballah, Qi Gong. We also invent our own American contemplative traditions or "New Age" practices like Unity, sound baths, and all varieties of energy healing. Americans reinvent the wheel over and over, with new proprietary names like Quantum Touch, Power of Eight, Remote Viewing, Wording, and Biofield Tuning.

There is massive societal support for a paradigm shift away from rigid materialist thinking, and people are moving on without academia. The market is flooded with subtle-energy practices that provide meaning for those who do them. However, mainstream society (e.g. public education) still obligates people to honor the denial of the Light Body. This is a new type of persecution where people are compelled to lead two different lives. Those who know their Light Body to be real are usually "in the closet" for fear of damaging their professional or personal reputation.

Understanding the Light Body to be a Human Universal and normalizing Light Body Theory is the framework needed to break out of this fear cycle. It legitimizes what we already know, and it places our society as one that is starting over. We're developing a new cultural heritage to understand our subtle-energy anatomy, while maintaining independence from the politics of religion.

Teachers learning about Light Body Intelligence provides a specific, practical example of this need. We need Light Body Theory for teachers to be supported to use subtle energy techniques for stress management in the classroom.

CHAPTER NINE

Light Body is Energy with Adaptation

In this section, I share my thought process to connect the dots between Brown's five points and the phenomena we see and experience.

I'll begin with my personal cosmology that allows me to understand the Light Body. It's my version of Adam and Eve or the Great Cosmic Turtle. My knowledge about the latest discoveries is far from complete, but I'm discovering new amazing things all the time.

Next, I'll recap the Stephens Gain Theorem and provide a slower, more detailed explanation of what it all means.

I hope this fuels your imagination.

MY COSMOLOGY

Everything in existence is made out of the same essential source energy, and it's all been moving ever since the Big Bang. I don't know if I really believe in the Big Bang, but it suits my understanding that energy moves and time passes.

Through the passage of time, vibrating energy takes on information that changes its state. That means it's subject to a process of evolution, and source energy has been differentiated into a variety of different states. We're familiar with the wave and particle states of electromagnetic light and matter, but I am certain that there are other states that we truly do not understand and we can't measure. I believe that consciousness is energy that exists in one of those states. Perhaps subtle energy (aka etheric energy) is another state.

If you visualize energy differentiation as a tree structure, then waves and particles would be on nearby branches. Subtle energy and consciousness, however, seem like completely different beasts, so they must be on a more distant section of the tree.

I found support for this idea in a Seth channeling by Jane Roberts:

> "Frameworks 1 and 2 obviously represent not only different kinds of reality in normal terms, but two different kinds of consciousness. To make this discussion as simple as possible for now, at least, think of these two frameworks or states of consciousness as being connected by "undifferentiated areas" in which sleep, dreaming, and certain trance states have their activity. Those undifferentiated areas are involved in the constant translation of one kind of consciousness into another, and with energy transferences,"[36]

Below is a diagram of my imagined phylogenetic tree that I assembled out of free clipart (Not AI). Please remember that it's very very hypothetical. It really doesn't matter on a practical level if it's right or wrong. It's just a theoretical answer that keeps me from wasting time trying to figure out things that are truly inscrutable.

---

[36] Roberts, Jane. (1981) *The Individual and the Nature of Mass Events*. Prentice Hall, p 113.

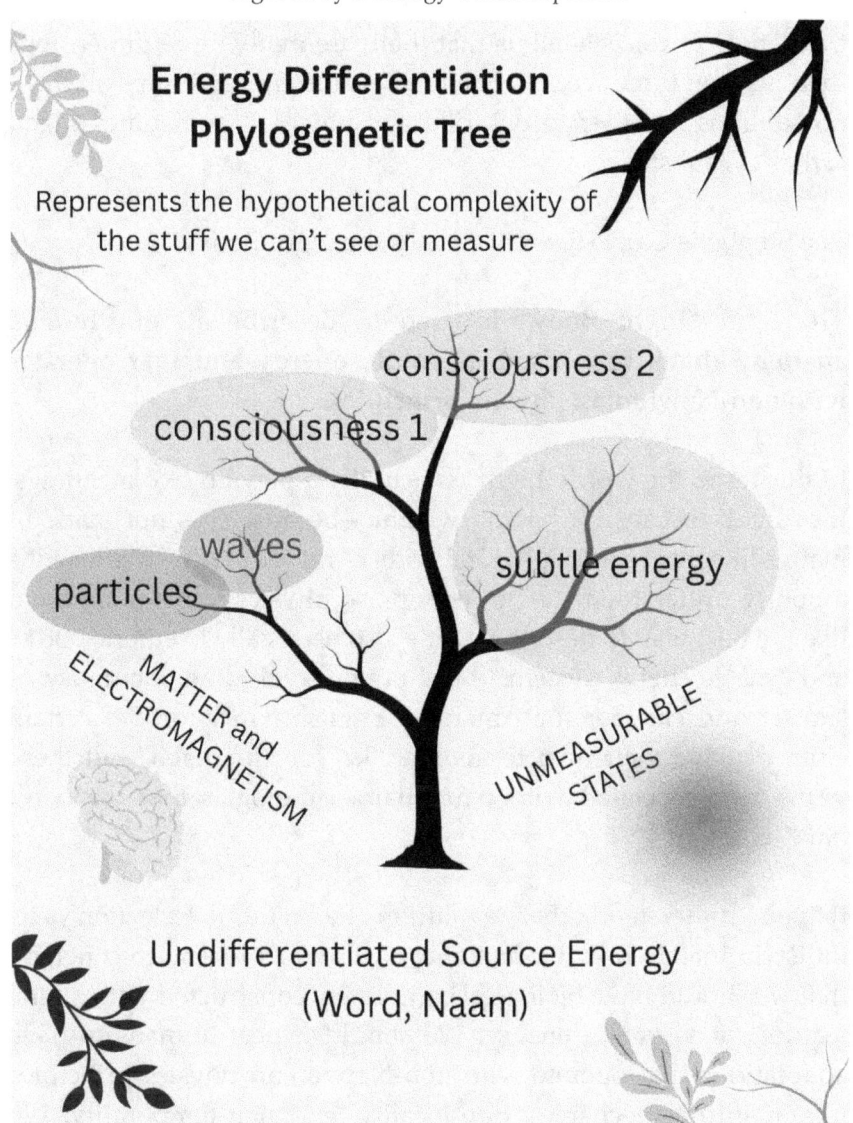

SUBTLE ENERGY AND NATURAL SELECTION

"Subtle Energy" is a term used to describe energy in states that are inscrutable to us humans. When you consider the evolution of biological complexity, it's important to keep in mind that there are more energy states than just waves and particles, there are more physical laws than the easy-to-understand "Newtonian" ones, and theoretical physicists tell us that there are many more dimensions than just the three we see. The term subtle energy lumps all these possibilities together to describe non-physical (sometimes called "etheric") substance.

The Stephens Gain Theorem defines the Light Body.

The term "Light Body" is used to describe all our human anatomy that's comprised of subtle energy and that operates with non-Newtonian physics principles.

In this term, the word "Light" is actually a play on two meanings. It's "light" because it has no weight - because it is not made of matter like our regular physical body. And it's "light" because it's a poorly understood state of energy, so physics terms often seem like the best way to describe it. It's also been called "etheric body" and "subtle energy system," but I prefer "Light Body" because its shorter and catchier for American English. In addition, certain cultures have their own terms like "ka" or "merkaba" but these terms are associated with particular cosmologies that we don't have to adopt.

If you understand that evolution by natural selection acts indiscriminately on vibrating energy, then it's logical to conclude that we should have biological complexity constructed with all the features of vibrating energy. We should expect humans to have adaptations that operate with non-Newtonian physics principles like quantum mechanics, non-locality, and non-temporality. We should also expect humans to have adaptations in higher-order-dimensions and different states of energy that we cannot easily see or understand, like dark matter or dark energy.

The current dominant ideology within Biological Science, however, assumes that natural selection prefers to act only within the three-dimensional, electrochemical, Newtonian physics properties of Deoxyribonucleic Acid. It feels natural and right to do that, but it is an outdated hegemony that Theoretical Physics is pressuring us to outgrow. I don't understand the math, but I trust that physicists know that there are real, non-local, non-temporal, multidimensional phenomena that we do not easily understand.

WHY IS SUBTLE ENERGY INVISIBLE?

"Subtle energy" is a general term for real energy existing in a physical state or dimensional state that is not a perfect match for the input parameters of our most salient cognitive capacities.

Evolutionary theory can explain why we find ourselves stuck with this limited world view. Our tunnel-vision to prioritize this certain subset of "reality" actually reveals the adaptive design of our intelligence systems. Some of our analytical systems (e.g. the innate physics demonstrated by newborns) evolved to operate with a specific spectrum of input to pay attention to wave/particle Newtonian-physics. Those must have been the systems that evolved further to form the building blocks of shared knowledge and culture.

The design of our perceptual system limits us to looking at our bodies and the world through matter. (That's actually mentioned on the list of Human Universals - classification of body parts, time, self-image, spacial cognition, social awareness of others). Infants perceive the world through innate physics, and it may be in infancy where the world of matter is created and maintained. Maybe Isaac Newton just described what human babies do, not the other way around.

TWICE THE COMPLEXITY

I hope you can see from the above discussion that the existence of the Light Body is supported by scientific theories of evolution through natural selection. It brings Biology up to date with the current state of Theoretical Physics (For example, the 2022 Nobel prize in Physics was awarded for non-locality!).

Beyond offering consilience between Theoretical Biology and Theoretical Physics, the idea of the Light Body actually expands what we can know about our bodies and ourselves. We can and should research our Light Body as an evolved intelligence system that performs functions for life and has been subject to natural selection. Throughout the evolutionary history of humans, selection pressures acted on the physical body and the Light Body at the same time.

Our human anatomy is at least twice as complex as materialist thought allows it to be. Every cell, every organ, and every system of the body has a Light Body component. Some Light Body components have the same adaptive function as a part of physical anatomy and could be described as an "interface" between physical and non-physical bodies. Other Light Body components could have adaptive functions that are unique to Non-Newtonian energy.

When smart people use the word "brain" interchangeably with "mind," "intelligence," or "consciousness" they're blinding themselves to at least half the picture. Our anatomical intelligence systems include both the mind-boggling complexity of the brain plus the mind-boggling complexity of our Light Bodies.

DENIAL OF THE LIGHT BODY IS A RELIGIOUS IDEA

If you work as a scientist or academic, it means you have agreed to join this coalition to secure your livelihood. As such, academics have shaped their Light Bodies to conform to the subtle-energy norms of their group. They have also adopted the beliefs of high-status elders to position themselves within a professional coalition that competes with other professional coalitions for the limited resources of public influence and financial support. Ironically, this is the type of social networking behavior described by academics trying to understand the adaptive function of religion. Therefore, denial of the Light Body by materialist scientific orthodoxy can be considered a religious idea.

HIGHER CONSCIOUSNESS

In addition to interfacing with our physical bodies, our Light Bodies are our interfaces with some form of "higher consciousness" that our human intelligence is not designed to understand.

Since we can't understand it, the historical status quo has been a long-standing agreement to ignore consciousness altogether so we don't fight about it. However, when materialist thinkers ignore consciousness, they also ignore a significant ability of human systems to move and change the consciousness that interfaces throughout our bodies.

What do I mean by change the consciousness that interfaces throughout our bodies? It's what we do every day when we go to sleep and wake up. There is abundant evidence in human behavior that the systems that determine our connections to consciousness can be manipulated in surprising ways. Hypnosis for surgical anesthesia is a dramatic example. Healing with subtle energy flowing through the hands is another example.

In addition, some people are skilled at self-manipulating their connections to consciousness to bring through "channeled" information from different sources of higher consciousness. This is called "trance," and some researchers explain trance to be the normal process whereby normal people move through different states of consciousness throughout their day.[37] Glossolalia (speaking in tongues) and channeling Light Language are examples of deliberate inner movement to change our connection to consciousness.[38]

How do we do it? We use our Light Bodies.

From my perspective, most of our best ideas, those that give us a self-identity, come from our "higher selves," and everyone is channeling all the time unless we're asleep, in a dissociative trance, anesthetized, or sleepwalking. (FYI, I would never take the drug Ambien. Yikes.)

There are countless books and lectures produced by reputable professional channelers that confirm that our ideas come from our connection to a source that transcends our physical bodies. In the next chapter, I'll introduce you to an important idea that came from a channeled source.

---

[37] Hope, Anna and Laurence Sugarman (2015) Orienting Hypnosis. *American Journal of Clinical Hypnosis* 57: 212-229.

[38] Newberg, Wintering, Morgan, and Waldman. (2006) The measurement of regional cerebral blood flow during glossolalia: A preliminary SPECT study. *Psychiatry Research: Neuroimaging* 148: 67–71.

Nicola Light (2025) *Pleiadian Handbook for Human Ascension: Inner Light Wisdom.* NicolaLight.com.

CHAPTER TEN
Earthization

"The basic source Aspect can't be actualized in this system because its reality is too big to fit. It *is* dominant at another level. But it has a living quality, patterned on our ideas of wisdom, super-existence and so forth, and is **earthized** in a personification that makes some kind of sense to us. Behind or within this personification is the being or consciousness that is so represented."

~ Jane Roberts[39]

The term Earthization was invented by Jane Roberts who channeled the Seth material in the mid-20th century. I consider her to be a true genius for her independent experimentation with consciousness and her lack of ego that so often tarnishes the information produced by professional channelers. Earthization is an important concept for Light Body Theory because it explains some of the variability we see between individuals and cultures.

There is energy and information that lie outside the scope of what our intelligence systems evolved to consciously perceive and

---

[39] Roberts, Jane (1975) *Adventures in Consciousness: An Introduction to Aspect Psychology*. Prentice-Hall.

understand. The electromagnetic spectrum of light is an obvious example. We can only see the range of frequencies from red to violet, but we know that other frequencies exist and other animals like bees can see them. We know that our bodies use some of the invisible frequencies to invisibly produce Vitamin D, and Vitamin D invisibly affects our health. We are aware of our health, but not of the light frequencies that influence it.

In a similar fashion, there is energy and information accessible to our Light Bodies that lie outside the scope of what our intelligence systems evolved to consciously perceive and understand. It is possible that the design of our bodies includes ways to use this energy and information in an invisible way (analogous the generation of Vitamin D). It is also possible for us to make this information accessible to our conscious awareness by using the idea of something invisible as a metaphor that connects it to our understanding of the physical world (or a comprehensible intermediary, like Vitamin D). That's Earthization.

Earthization is a way to use unintelligible information from inscrutable realms by converting it into a system that makes sense for humans living on Earth. If Earthization is a Human Universal, as I believe it is, then it explains why humans have invented a vast variety of ways to use Non-Newtonian information.

If you deny the possibility of Earthization, as many academics feel obligated to do, then you're restricting your imagination of the vast complexities of human potential.

In the United States, Remote Viewing is an example of Earthization. So is ESP (Extra Sensory Perception), and so is prayer. Reiki and Quantum Touch are Earthizations for healing. Earthization is performed in music performances. Earthization is performed in tarot card readings. Earthization is performed with William Tiller's intention devices and PEAR's Random Event Generators (REGs). Earthization is performed in sound healing and Biofield Tuning. Earthization is performed when I make a glass penguin into a talisman for feeling your Light Body. The list goes on and on.

LIGHT BODY THEORY IS PRACTICAL

Light Body Theory incorporates logic with lived experience, and it allows us to be where we are in our ignorance about what lies beyond human comprehension. We don't have to agree about consciousness to see that accepting the Light Body to be real is a practical way to use more of our human capacity. You're already using it, so you might as well use it purposefully while we wait for science to catch up.

If you take your Light Body seriously, you will be surprised at what it does for you and what you can do with it. You can feel your Light Body because your physical body and Light Body interface with each other - they work together. The Light Body has structure much like the organs in our physical bodies. The structure, however, operates differently than matter; yet it functions in the normal processes of life like homeostasis, metabolism, socialization, and learning. You move your Light Body, but it's not the three-dimensional type of movement that we are accustomed to understand.

Love your Light Body. Love yourself.

CHAPTER ELEVEN

A Summary

In this chapter, I'll review how to apply this foundational framework to understand Light Body variability. I hope you'll see how this approach leads to useful, sometimes surprising, insights about how modern environments may be influencing people today.

Non-physical traits that are Human Universals feature:

1 - A Method of Reproduction or Replication.

2 - Parameter-setting learning mechanisms.

3 - Maternal/family imprinting in infancy.

4 - Critical learning periods in childhood when environmental exposure shapes development.

5 - Lifelong adaptability and skill development through cultural learning.

6 - Modern expression of the trait operates with Adaptive Design based on ancestral evolutionary history.

7 - Novel environments that are different from the Environment of Evolutionary Adaptedness (EEA) can produce novel traits and behaviors that might seem maladaptive. (In other words, Adaptive Design does NOT mean maximizing fitness.) The novel environment is called an Evolutionary Mismatch.

EXAMPLE - LANGUAGE

Next, I'll give a familiar example to show you how to apply this theory to understand a complex trait.

Language is a Human Universal, so we can examine these features to understand why we see variability in the languages that are spoken by humans worldwide.[40]

1 - A Method of Reproduction or Replication: All humans are born with potential to learn and speak language.

2 - Parameter-setting learning mechanisms: Infants instinctively listen to the spoken language in their environments, and they babble as they acquire the grammatical foundation for a particular language.

3 - Maternal/family imprinting in infancy: Exposure to the family's language sets the individual's native phonemes, and they learn the accent of the location they were born into. For example, Japanese speakers lose the ability to distinguish between the sounds "r" and "l", but English speakers retain this ability.

4 - Developmental Learning Periods in Childhood: Children learn languages, including second languages, easier and more

---

[40] For a discussion of the evolutionary psychology of language, see Pinker, Steven (2025 update) *The Language Instinct: How the Mind Creates Language*. Harper. (originally published in 1994)

thoroughly than adults. For example, creoles are complete native languages that are spoken by children whose parents speak pidgin, an incomplete second language they learned as an adult.

5 - Lifelong adaptability and skill development through cultural learning: Adults can learn second-languages by studying them. Spoken accents can change when someone moves to a different location or experiences a significant social change.

6 - Modern expression of the trait operates with Adaptive Design based on the ancestral evolutionary history: It is understood that Language evolved due to the selection pressures experienced by our Hunter-Gatherer ancestors in the Pleistocene Epoch.

7 - Novel environments that are different from the Environment of Evolutionary Adaptedness (EEA) can produce novel traits and behaviors that might seem maladaptive. (In other words, Adaptive Design does NOT mean maximizing fitness.) The novel environment is called an Evolutionary Mismatch.

Language evolved for in-person, spoken communication long before recording technology was invented, so audio recordings of spoken language are an Evolutionary Mismatch for the Adaptive Design of our Language intelligence systems. Exposure to audio recordings of language might produce novel traits and behaviors.

For example, the technological development of broadcast radio and news created a "neutral" English accent. This accent could be considered novel because it is not associated with a physical location and it's spoken by a vastly larger population than those of the pre-technological communities relevant to the EEA.

A Summary
LIGHT BODY HUMAN UNIVERSAL

Finally, we'll examine these features to reveal possible explanations for why we see variability among the Light Body expression of people worldwide.

1 - A Method of Reproduction or Replication: All humans are born with Non-Newtonian anatomy. Light Bodies may differ in heritable ways relevant to biological human reproduction.

2 - Parameter-setting learning mechanisms: Newborns may instinctively pay attention to subtle energy and Light Body activity in their environment. They may replicate that activity through practice and resonance.

3 - Maternal/family imprinting in infancy: Exposure to maternal and familial Light Bodies may shape the infant's Light Body in a foundational way. A relevant parameter could be how we move our Light Bodies in and out of a normal resting state. Another parameter could be the extent that we Listen, Sing, and Witness with our Light Bodies in tandem with physical behaviors. We could expect maternal Light Body imprinting to be particularly influential because of the long gestation period.

4 - Developmental Learning Periods in Childhood: Children may be sensitized to learn the cultural norms for Light Body behavior in their native environments. This learning could become integrated in a lifelong foundational way analogous to a native language. Socialization from childhood through puberty would be a significant time where Light Body interactions with peers would inform self-identity.

5 - Lifelong adaptability and skill development through cultural learning: Adults can develop Light Body skills through a variety of mental focus and perceptual practices including meditation, prayer, yoga, Qi Gong, Reiki, remote viewing, subtle-energy

healing with hands, music listening, music performance, sound editing/recording...

6 - Modern expression of the trait operates with Adaptive Design based on the ancestral evolutionary history: Our Light Body Intelligence systems evolved due to the selection pressures experienced by our Hunter-Gatherer ancestors in the Pleistocene Epoch.

7 - Novel environments that are different from the Environment of Evolutionary Adaptedness (EEA) can produce novel traits and behaviors that might seem maladaptive. (In other words, Adaptive Design does NOT mean maximizing fitness.) The novel environment is called an Evolutionary Mismatch.

Our Light Body Intelligence Systems evolved for in-person interactions before recording technology was invented, so audio and video recordings are an Evolutionary Mismatch for the Adaptive Design of our Light Body Intelligence systems. This will be discussed in detail in later chapters.

Part Three

A Model of the Light Body

E. Stephens Gain

CHAPTER TWELVE
A Theoretical Model

In Parts I and II, I met you where you were. I held your hand, and we baby-stepped out of the cold, barren tundra together. In Part III, we've hopped on a plane and arrived somewhere sunny and warm.

In this section, I'm going to tell you about my working model of the Light Body as an Intelligence System. I say "working" because this is what makes sense based on how I operate in my daily life. I'm indebted to a variety of teachers and the energetic techniques I've studied and experimented with for over thirty some years. I'm doing my best to organize and explain how everything I know from experience and study converge into a sensible system.

This section is theoretical, and I'm not in a position to do formal, in-depth hypothesis testing on my model. If you are equipped to do that, then I hope this section inspires you to experiment with these ideas. Tell me if you figure out something interesting.

One of my goals here is to provide a working model for people who are ready to use Light Body Intelligence in a public or professional way. This will justify energy healing practitioners of all kinds, and it will validate many of the ways we experience music and religion. It will provide a theoretical foundation for teachers to use subtle-energy techniques for stress management (I call them Lightworkers in Classrooms). In my view, anyone who has made it to top ranks of their profession is already using Light Body Intelligence, so let's acknowledge this reality now.

Another of my goals is to get technology developers and public policy makers to understand why I think social media and AI interfaces could damage individuals and society in ways that are yet to be recognized. Could our societal ignorance of the Light Body be weaponized against us? Please take this seriously and help me answer that question.

LIGHT BODY IS A HUMAN BODY

With Light Body Theory, Light Bodies are extensions of our physical bodies. We have a physical hand and a Light Body hand. We have physical lungs and Light Body lungs. We have a physical brain and a Light Body brain.

Light Body Intelligence is built into all our bodily systems. From an evolutionary standpoint, Light Body adaptations can be understood to solve the same adaptive problems we consider when we discuss the underlying design of human anatomy or the human mind. I'll broadly outline this way of thinking with the list of assumptions below. These are points to keep in mind throughout the discussions in later chapters.

Diversity

In the same way that human bodies are not all the same, there is diversity among Light Bodies. Inheritance, developmental influences, environmental factors, and experience create this diversity.

Relatedness

People who are related in some way (e.g. within families, tribes, or speaking the same language) have similarities in their Light Bodies, and we have social intelligence to detect this relatedness.

Movement

We move our Light Bodies constantly, in parallel with moving our physical bodies. Light Body movement must be understood in a new way because it's Non-Newtonian.

Perception

We perceive information about our environment with our Light Bodies, in tandem with perceiving with our physical bodies. Light Body perception must be understood in a new way because it's Non-Newtonian.

Communication

We communicate with our Light Bodies, in tandem with communicating with our physical bodies. Light Body communication must be understood in a new way because it's Non-Newtonian.

Cooperation

Light Body Intelligence is a significant part of our species' ability to cooperate. Social bonding, group building, conflict avoidance, and behavior are coordinated in Non-Newtonian ways.

Coalitions

Light Body Intelligence is a significant part of our Coalitional Intelligence to form loyal groups that compete with other groups.

CHAPTER THIRTEEN

How do we Move our Light Bodies?

We can *Earthize* our understanding of Non-Newtonian anatomy by visualizing the Light Body to be an invisible, egg-shaped bubble that surrounds and penetrates the physical body. I imagine it looks like the glass penguin photographed on the front cover of this book. Visualizing it can help you see how we move it.

There are many ways we deliberately *move* our Light Bodies.

THREE-DIMENSIONAL MOVEMENT

We can move our Light Body in three-dimensional space. We can pull in the edges of the Light Body bubble, so our energy is tight around our body. I'll describe what this feels like to me. When I do this, it takes some effort to pull it in tight, and it is a bit uncomfortable and claustrophobic.

When you stop pulling in the Light Body bubble, you "relax" it, so it fills whatever size is normal for you. The normal size has been described as three to six feet around your body, but people vary greatly in size.

How do we Move our Light Bodies?

You can expand your Light Body to take up more space around your body than it usually does. You can purposefully stretch it out to fill a room, a house, the planet, or bigger. In my experience, it will bounce back to normal size without sustained effort.

Light Bodies expand and contract automatically depending on the situation and the environment. If someone pulls more of their "higher self" into their bodies, the size of their Light Body grows. Multiple times I have been surprised to feel the Light Body of someone in an adjacent room expanding through the walls when they began meditation. It felt like a wave passing through my body. I also feel Light Bodies expand when someone displays their expertise, as when I asked a salesperson in Sur La Table a question about knives, her favorite section of the store. I am sure that the Light Bodies of performers of all kinds expand in significant ways, but I am usually too distracted by the performance to notice.

Some people naturally have an extra-potent Light Body and it can have an extra-strong effect on others, even when they're not intending to do anything. I call this having a *Big* Light Body because some invisible quality about it is greater than other, normal sized Light Bodies.

Sometimes people act defensively toward people with Big Light Bodies because they're convinced they were provoked, but they're actually mis-interpreting the large-size as a threat. An analogy would be if a ten-foot-tall person joins a group of normal-sized strangers, one of them is bound to feel scared and act out. People with Big Light Bodies are surprised to be the target of seemingly irrational, defensive aggression every now and then. (Guess how I know.)[41]

---

[41] I also know that some readers of this book have Big Light Bodies, and they will be greatly relieved by my interpretation.

VIBRATIONAL MOVEMENT

Our Light Bodies are Non-Newtonian, so we can move them in ways that you might not typically think of as movement. People use the term "vibration" to describe a state of subtle energy and the particular information that it holds. We can *move* our Light Bodies vibrationally from one vibration to another.

Most people are aware of perceiving Light Body vibration as a "gut feeling" that they don't understand. It takes practice to learn how to discern Light Body vibrations and move vibrationally at will.

Vibrational states can be felt along a spectrum from "low" to "high," and they can also hold complex qualitative information that I describe as feeling like a "flavor" in your Light Body. Low feels bad like fear or stifling malaise, and high feels bright, tingly, and has an electric charge to it. Vibrational flavors can be simple like the idea of a color or a feeling, or complex like a phrase, a story, or even an abstract idea.

When you think about moving the Light Body in vibration, a useful metaphor is an audio interface. You can imagine having virtual EQ "knobs" (e.g. bass, treble, mid) to adjust the vibration, making spectral high-low adjustments and qualitative "flavor" adjustments.

A common way to move your light body vibrationally from one flavor to another is by saying "I Am" affirmations and *doing* them in a performative way. "I am blue." "I am green." "I am love." "I am gratitude." You can be more precise by using the word, "through." [42] "I am blue through my Light Body." "I am love

---

[42] The "I Am… through" technique is taught in Paul Selig's channeled books, *I Am the Word* (2010), *The Book of Love and Creation* (2012) and *The Book of Knowing and Worth* (2013). This technique is also a precise way to do Witnessing, a Light Body behavior which will be discussed

How do we Move our Light Bodies?

through my Light Body." "I am gratitude through my Light Body." "I am all the digits in pi through my Light Body." "I am the United States Constitution through my Light Body." "I am a peanut butter sandwich through my Light Body."

It should be noted that using language is not required to move your Light Body vibrationally. Using I Am affirmations is an Earthization that enables you to deliberately do Non-Newtonian movements that you already do. Many people are skilled at moving vibrationally without language.

In addition, the vibrational "flavors" don't have to be translatable into words, they can be unsymbolic. Our use of unsymbolic information is poorly understood. Unsymbolic thought is rarely researched because it is intractable to our consciousness awareness.

An analogy to explain unsymbolic vibrational movement is to imagine an array of electronic oscillators in an old-school music synthesizer. Turning the effect knobs changes the shape and configuration of electronic sine waves, creating new waves with complexity that is seemingly infinite. When the output waves are converted to sound, we're unable to hear a large portion of this complexity because our auditory systems are optimized to process the sounds relevant to human speech and physical environments (frequencies between 20 Hz to 20,000 Hz).[43] The unperceivable complexity in the electronic wave is analogous to the unsymbolic vibrational information used by our Light Bodies.

---

in the next chapter.

[43] Cymatics is a way to visualize unhearable electronic complexity by allowing grains of sand to form patterns on a vibrating plate.

CHANNELS AND SIGNAL FLOW

There is yet another significant way we move our Light Bodies. We do a type of internal movement to change our body's access to conscious awareness and the flow of information between the lower-dimensional matter of our physical bodies and the higher-dimensional energies of consciousness. Returning to the mixing board metaphor, you can visualize this as turning the dials that route the input and output signals and gain.

This is one of the mysteries of consciousness that everyone can do, yet no one knows how we do it. I'm going to give a list of real-world examples to clarify what this Light Body movement is.

The difference between asleep and awake is the most obvious and ubiquitous example of this kind of Light Body movement. Using the mixing board analogy, some of the signal flow between consciousness and the physical body becomes disconnected during sleep. This signal re-routing displays evidence of evolutionarily adaptive design.[44]

Another obvious example is a person experienced with channeling[45] who moves internal dials, and a completely different personality speaks through her body about topics that are unknown to her when she's not in a trance state. The channeler ends the session by re-setting the internal dials so the signal from her normal self controls her body.

There is a variety of less obvious ways we move the signal routing of our Light Bodies. What is known about hypnosis and trance provides clues to this movement. Some researchers theorize that

---

[44] Symons, Donald (1993). The stuff that dreams aren't made of: Why wake-state and dream-state sensory experiences differ. *Cognition* 47(3): 181-217.

[45] See *Adventures in Consciousness* (1975) by Jane Roberts who channels Seth for a description and analysis of the experience of channeling.

hypnosis is adaptive inner state change arising from a primitive "orienting reflex."[46] Hypnosis for surgical anesthesia and sleepwalking are similar types of inner state changes.

Many examples of human behavior support the idea that changing the signal routing of consciousness is normal and adaptive.[47] Research on glossolalia reveals that anyone can learn to deliberately partition their awareness to allow our voices and bodies to move without conscious control, and it *feels good* to do so.[48] Energetic healing modalities like Reiki and Quantum Touch involve an inner state change to allow the flow of healing energy and unsymbolic information, and this *feels good* too. People who speak and express Light Language also experience pleasurable inner feelings from this inner state change.[49]

Partitioning conscious awareness can be understood as a Light Body signal-routing movement, and the ability to do it can be developed as a skill. People who are professional listeners, court reporters, sound mixers, and dialogue editors have trained their listening attention to separate the quality of the sound from the semantic content of words. This is similar to some meditation practices like the Lamaze pain control technique to pay attention to two different focus points to distract from labor pain.

---

[46] Hope and Sugarman (2015). Orienting Hypnosis. *American Journal of Clinical Hypnosis*, 57:212-229.

[47] Lynn, Christopher (2005). Adaptive and Maladaptive Dissociation: An Epidemiological and Anthropological Comparison and Proposition for an Expanded Dissociation Model. *Anthropology of Consciousness* 16(2): 16-50.

[48] Kildahl, John P (1972). *The Psychology of Speaking in Tongues*. Harper & Row.
  Sherrill, John L. (1964) *They Speak with Other Tongues*. Chosen Books.

[49] Dent, Alexandra (2025). Soul Level Healing and Light Language chapter in *Using Spirituality in EMDR Therapy*. Routledge.

For all these examples that I describe as Light Body signal-routing movements, mainstream science has a poor understanding of what people are doing. For example, it's mostly unknown why people don't remember trance or dream experiences, but sometimes they do. EEGs of people channeling look the same as people who are not channeling.[50] Light Body Theory offers a new approach to attempt to sort this out.

FOCUS OF ATTENTION

The Light Body is surely involved when we change the focus of our attention. At this point, however, my observations about how we might perform this type of movement are vague and abstract.

Using the audio mixing metaphor, I imagine the focus of attention to be a complex effect like a compressor, and dials can be moved to change the parameters of a property of consciousness that's like density. I also observe that people vary greatly in their capacity to do this movement and in their normal *resting density*. The "big" Light Body phenomenon I described previously could be related to differences in what I'm calling resting density. It's a big mystery.

---

[50] Wahbeh H, Cannard C, Okonsky J, Delorme A. A physiological examination of perceived incorporation during trance. F1000Res. 2019 Jan 17;8:67.

CHAPTER FOURTEEN

Light Body Behaviors

What do we do with our Light Bodies?

I've analyzed my own Light Body experiences in view of what's known about human intelligence, and I say that we have a Light Body Intelligence System because our Light Bodies do things with information. This intelligence operates in tandem with the Newtonian-centric intelligence systems we are more comfortable discussing, intelligence that's hypothesized to emerge solely from the activity of brain matter.

I've categorized what we do with our Light Bodies into the catalogue of behaviors described below. I propose that these are Universal Light Body behaviors, and I challenge researchers to investigate this claim. By organizing them in this way, I hope to provide a new framework that can be used to explore other phenomena.

PASSIVE BEHAVIORS

Being

To Be is the embodied presence of information in the Light Body that can be detected by other individuals. Adaptively, this is what a Light Body "looks like" to another Light Body. It's the information a clairvoyant psychic "reads" when focusing on someone's Light Body. Among psychic traditions, it is assumed that this information is simple and honest. Adaptively, however, sharing information about the self would have been subject to evolutionary selection pressures analogous to other biologically relevant phenomena like signaling, camouflage, status and tribal affiliation markers.

Knowing

To Know is the embodied presence of something that is Believed. Knowing is the Light Body storing information as a vibrational pattern it can use. When semantic "believing" is performative (i.e. it does something), it programs the Light Body to Know. "I Am" statements are commonly used to program the Light Body to know.

Resonating

The Light Body automatically aligns to the ambient vibration in its environment. This can be called attunement. The environment attunes the Light Body. The Light Body will passively resonate with the vibration of its environment unless effort is put forth to prevent that vibrational movement. It's like the Light Body's virtual EQ knobs are automatically adjusted by the environment.

Resonating to the Mean

When a Light Body is in a group of Light Bodies that hold a variety of different vibrational states, it will automatically align to a group vibration that takes into account information from the space and from all the Light Bodies in the group. All Light Bodies in the group will gravitate toward this vibrational mean unless effort is put forth to prevent that vibrational movement.

In a safe space (like a classroom), a group has an "average vibration" that everyone automatically resonates with. Some individuals can influence this group average more than others. Individuals can "shield" themselves to prevent themselves from resonating with the group average or attempt to "push" the group average to a higher or lower vibration. It takes effort to resist resonating to the mean, and a person who is obligated by their job to do so (e.g. a schoolteacher) will tire from doing it all day.

ACTIVE BEHAVIORS

Deep Listening

I use the term "Deep Listening" to describe how we listen with our Light Bodies. We focus our attention to obtain subtle-energy information from an intended target. Subtle-energy information is *unsymbolic*. It is not words or images, and for the most part, we cannot translate the information into words or images if we try. (It's Earthization when we translate unsymbolic subtle-energy information into words or images. Remote Viewing is an example of Deep Listening with translation. Remote Viewing is an emic expression of Deep Listening.)

Deep Listening is normal, everyday "psychic" behavior that usually goes unnoticed. It's important to think about how this capacity could have evolved. From an adaptive standpoint, our ability to do Deep Listening must have improved the survival and reproduction of our human ancestors.

We need to think about the adaptive problems Deep Listening would have solved in our ancestral environments to understand the design of the phenomena we see today. Scientists call this the Environment of Evolutionary Adaptedness, the EEA.[51] The EEA for Deep Listening did not have phones, broadcast radio,

---

[51] Tooby, John and Leda Cosmides (1990). The past explains the present: Emotional adaptations and the structure of ancestral environments. *Ethology and Sociobiology*, 11, 375-424.

television, sound recording, video recording, or any of our modern communication technologies. Therefore, our human Light Body capacity to do Deep Listening must necessarily be designed for local relationships in societies that lacked reliable long-distance communication.

Light Body Singing

Light Body Singing is a behavior to broadcast subtle-energy vibrational information. It's different from Being because it's a type of Light Body manipulation (could be called a trance) to radiate information out of the Light Body. Some people program their Light Body (Being) to Sing all the time, usually in high vibrational frequency (Christ consciousness is an example). Many people Sing with their Light Bodies when they sing with their voices, and I believe that Light Body Singing is a poorly understood goal of most singers and singing performances. Some people Sing with their Light Bodies when they write or create art.

Light Body Singing feels good in our physical bodies, and it's often understood to be a flow of energy from higher states of consciousness into matter. In my view, glossolalia is Light Body Singing that is triggered by the physical act of vocalization. A Light Body signal-flow *movement* has disconnected the symbolic function of speech so the voice is activated to Sing with the Light Body. Subtle energy healing modalities like Reiki and Quantum Touch involve a similar signal-flow change to bypass symbolic thought.

The adaptive function of Light Body Singing is related to the adaptive function of Light Body Listening. Taken together, they comprise Light Language which should be appreciated as a complex communication system analogous with spoken language.

Witnessing

Witnessing is a Light Body behavior that takes place where two Light Bodies overlap. One Light Body "imagines" the other

Light Body vibrating with a different frequency or flavor than the other Light Body's vibration currently holds. I use the word "imagine" loosely because Witnessing takes effort. The effort feels like reaching out to the space occupied by another Light Body and exerting a muscular force to lift a heavy weight. Doing so changes the subtle energy environment for that Light Body, inviting it to resonate with the frequency or flavor that is being imagined. It must be noted that Witnessing is ubiquitous to all kinds of relationships. Witnessing can occur in a beneficial way, in a harmful way, or even in a neutral, labeling way.

Witnessing has been taught throughout history in esoteric, mystical, and religious practices. Whenever it's taught, the particular vocabulary used to teach it tends to become proprietary to the teacher and coalitional to the tribe of learners. If a teaching about Witnessing has been around a long time, it's usually become a religion or mystery school. If the teaching is a new reinvention of the wheel, appreciative students may succumb to guru-worship, and it starts looking like a cult. Light Body Theory provides an alternative to learn and teach about Witnessing that avoids these pitfalls.

Witnessing is an "etic" function of our human anatomy, but not all cultures have an "emic" representation of how we do it. In cultures of Roman-Empire descent (like the US), we have an "emic" idea that only a few special people can Witness. This can be explained because our culture descended from Roman Catholic law that a hierarchy of priests are the only people who can perform communion (a type of Witnessing). The idea that Witnessing only belongs to the few is still being reinforced through books, television shows, and movies like *Harry Potter*, *Avatar the Last Airbender*, and *The Matrix*.

Allowing
With sustained effort, the act of Witnessing usually results in the Witnessed Light Body moving in vibration to Resonate with

what is being Witnessed. I call that Allowing. Allowing can be an easy way to move in vibration because it's like passive environmental resonance. Allowing is different, however, because it is a social interaction, so the person doing the Witnessing must be trusted to some degree.

Amplifying

In a group setting, a person can allow their Light Body to resonate with a focus and flow that is determined externally by the group. In a functional way, this forms a Collective of synchronized Light Bodies that augment the group's vibration like the way electromagnetic waves combine to form a laser beam. Collectives have some of the same features as individual Light Bodies, but with a larger, *Amplified* energetic size and power.

People experience pleasure when they use their Light Bodies to Amplify a shared group focus. This is most easily experienced when we're in an audience listening to music or a performance of any kind. Amplification is performed in sports teams and work crews, and these examples demonstrate why I consider Amplification to be an adaptive mechanism that evolved to enable human Cooperation and Coalitional competition. I'll discuss that in Chapter 16.

CHAPTER FIFTEEN

Light Body Memory and Homeostasis

Researchers in cognitive science categorize different types of human memory based on the different ways we store, use, and retrieve information,[52] but there is one type of memory that they usually ignore. It's a memory stored in our bodies after we have emotional experiences. We feel different after something intense happens. With time, however, that feeling usually goes away, the memory gets cleared. I call this Light Body Memory, and I see it as two opposing systems that maintain a homeostatic balance to calibrate our emotional readiness for current circumstances.

The easiest way to see this memory system is with an extreme example. Soldiers returning from war have PTSD because their bodies have become "programmed" to expect extreme danger. Their brains, endocrine systems, and their Light Bodies have been calibrated so they are ready to act in a way that would be adaptive if there were a continued presence of extreme danger. Somatic therapy for PTSD recognizes that trauma is "stored in the body," and methods are prescribed to "clear" or "release" the body's

---

[52] Klein, Stanley, Cosmides L, Gangi CE, Jackson B, Tooby J, and Costabile KA. (2009). Evolution and Episodic Memory: An Analysis and Demonstration of a Social Function of Episodic Recollection. *Social Cognition* 27(2): 283-319.

memory imprint of that trauma. The memory imprint is in the Light Body.

We can also see this memory system in more moderate examples that many people are familiar with. After a stressful period of time, someone might get "bodywork," energy healing, or even a therapeutic massage in hopes of feeling better. During the treatment, the intuitive therapist might discover "stuck emotions" and focus their efforts on clearing them. To the person receiving the treatment, the release of this memory pattern might feel like a short-lived wave of sadness with tears for something long forgotten. To someone who feels their Light Body, the release may be experienced as a cloud of "dense" energy that becomes unstuck and moves through and out of the body. Pain in the body can sometimes be resolved immediately through Light Body Memory clearing like this.[53]

As demonstrated in the examples above, Light Body Memory involves two systems. One system *encodes* a pattern into the Light Body based on emotional lived experience. The other system *neutralizes* the pattern, and it operates in a mysterious way that's not as fast or as automatic as we would like it to be.

This perspective has broad potential to elucidate many unexplained phenomena of human experience. In the above examples, the encoded pattern was a bad-feeling emotion, and the neutralizing system needed a boost to return the Light Body to a comfortable, balanced state. If you understand this is an adaptive calibration system, then good-feeling or benign emotions would also get encoded because Light Body patterns reflect the endless variety of lived experiences. In most circumstances, the

---

[53] When I began studying psychic development thirty years ago, I was delighted to experience an unexpected release of pain that had been diagnosed as IBS by conventional doctors.

neutralizing system would be constantly and automatically sculpting our Light Body patterning without our noticing.

Evidence that there is a Light Body Memory encoding system can be found in the work of intuitives. Some accomplished modern examples are the medical intuitive Caroline Myss[54] and Eileen Day McKusick[55] who used tuning forks in an ingenious new way to map what she calls the Human Biofield. From a channeled perspective, a detailed description of "Soul Books" (an Earthization) stored in the human energy field can be found in a chapter channeled by Lee Harris.[56]

Evidence that there is a Light Body Memory neutralizing system can be found in the countless variety of energy healing modalities known throughout human history.[57] Pythagoras, the ancient Greek philosopher physician, performed "soul adjustments" with sound and music. In the late 1700s, the German physician Franz Mesmer established a popular movement to heal with what he called, "animal magnetism."

If you research the historical record about Mesmerism, you will discover practices analogous to modern hands-on healing

---

[54] Myss, Caroline (1996) *Anatomy of the Spirit: The Seven Stages of Power and Healing*. Harmony Books.

[55] McKusick, Eileen Day (2021) *Tuning the Human Biofield: Healing with Vibrational Sound Therapy* (Revised and Updated Edition). Healing Arts Press.

[56] Harris, Lee and Dianna Edwards (2025) *Conversations With the Z's: Book Three: Demystifying the Journey of Life Before and After Death.* Ch 4.

[57] It is also discussed in channeled literature, as in this quote from Seth through Jane Roberts: "It is true that dreams allow the physically oriented self to digest current experience, but it is also true that the experience is then returned to its initial components. It breaks apart, so to speak. Portions of it are retained as "past" physical sense data, but the whole experience returns to its initial direct state." P 81-82 *Seth Speaks*. (1972/1994) New World Library.

modalities like Reiki, Quantum Touch, and the Bengston Energy Healing Method. In the 1800s, Mesmerism could be easily learned from a book and practiced at home.[58] It's also notable that Mesmer clinics employed group healing sessions, which would have amplified their potency in accordance with modern experimental data on group coherence by PEAR Random Event Generators and Lynne McTaggart's Power of Eight groups.[59]

I propose that many religious practices and rituals activate the Light Body Memory clearing system. Some examples include certain types of prayer, Christ sanctification, and glossolalia. Amplification of clearings is evoked in many ways through rituals like singing, listening to music together, and chanting--ways in which a shared focus of intention creates Light Body vibrational coherency among individuals in the group. The clearing effect of these practices can explain the pleasurable feelings of wellness often reported after participating in religious services.

There are also many non-religious practices that activate the Light Body clearing system, including attending live music performances, singing, feeling the effects of singing bowls, and catharsis from attending artistic performances. Another example comes from people who speak, sing, and express "Light Language" through art and bodily movement.[60] This is a growing trend that is interpreted to be channeling unsymbolic energetic information. It is remarkably similar to glossolalia and mesmerism, including the fact that it feels good to channel it.

I consider all the examples above to be different ways of Earthizing the Light Body Memory system, which is the

---

[58] Martineau, Harriet (1845). *Miss Martineau's Letters on Mesmerism*. Harper & Brothers.
[59] McTaggart, Lynne (2017). *The Power of Eight*. Atria.
[60] I suggest doing an internet search for "light language". If you've never heard of it, you will be surprised.

underlying Human Universal. Grappling with the idea that there is a complex memory system to program and deprogram the Light Body in an adaptive way inspires me to imagine fascinating possibilities.

One possibility is that Light Body Memory contains a vast array of inherited information, including direct ancestral cellular memory patterns of a non-genetic, multi-dimensional kind. This could explain the perpetual "past life" influences that people who do psychic hygiene are compelled to clear like peeling an onion.

Another possibility is that encoded patterns in the Light Body may not only be neutralized in a mysterious way, but they may be re-programmed with new information in a mysterious way.

Based on personal experience, I know that our Light Bodies use information in ways that are yet to be identified. I hypothesize that we have evolved faculties to transfer unsymbolic information from one Light Body to another. This is a brave new world that has yet to be explored. That's why I'm exploring it through my work as a Light Language Recording Artist.

CHAPTER SIXTEEN
Social Intelligence

An adaptationist perspective gives us a way to tease apart the design of the Light Body using what we know about human evolution. Social intelligence is one of the hallmarks of our species,[61] so Light Body Intelligence must enable social intelligence in a significant way.

The adaptive design of any system of intelligence is revealed by analyzing how it uses information. In accordance with the principles of evolutionary psychology, humans have specific *mental mechanisms* to use information to solve problems that our ancestors experienced over a long span of time. Therefore, Light Body Intelligence can be understood by analyzing how we use information to solve "adaptive problems."[62]

In this chapter, I will provide an overview of this framework applied to four broad categories of social intelligence that have a

---

[61] Pagel, Mark. (2012) *Wired for Culture: Origins of the human social mind*. Norton.

[62] For a discussion of adaptive design and the methods evolutionary psychologists use to research it, see Barkow, Cosmides, & Tooby (Eds) (1992) *The Adapted Mind: Evolutionary Psychology and the Generation of Culture*. Oxford University Press.

significant Light Body component. I'll provide examples of how we experience the Light Body in ways that are in accordance with its adaptive design.

SAFETY

People are intelligent and resourceful, and they can be wonderful creative partners; but if you're near the wrong person at the wrong time, they can also be dangerous or even deadly. This has been a fundamental problem for our ancestors throughout human history. People need to know whom they can trust.

Our social intelligence is comprised of mechanisms for gathering information about other people and using that information to decide if they can be trusted. That's a fancy way of saying that certain things grab our attention when we first meet someone. What people look like, the way they dress, the way they speak, and the way they move their bodies are visible examples of information we use in this way. We also use information that is not visible like what's known about their relationships or their personal history. All this and more are considered to determine the extent that someone can be trusted, especially if it is a new person, a stranger you just met.

Light Body Intelligence contributes to help solve this adaptive problem. We perceive the vibrational status of another person's Light Body, and this information is used to assess a potential ally or enemy. We use this information in countless other ways as well, but from an evolutionary standpoint, safety is a very primitive adaptive problem. Our ancestors would have needed to solve basic social safety issues long before more complex social intelligence could have evolved. This adaptive function of Light Body Intelligence is foundational to maintaining safe family relationships and all types of social bonding and friendships.

People use this type of Light Body Intelligence all the time without noticing it. When people do notice it, they might describe having a gut-feeling about a person, or a hair-raising fear of someone. People report intuitively knowing something is wrong at the time when a family member was hurt or in danger.[63] Light Body perception is lumped together with visual cues. We usually give visual information full credit for informing our feelings, but we trust our Light Body perception without understanding what we're doing.

Becoming aware of Light Body information is a skill that can be developed through meditation and other practices that require sustained focus of non-visual attention.[64] A minority of people who are commonly described as "psychics" and "energy readers" can translate the vibrational information perceived about other people's Light Bodies into visualizations and speech. Certain techniques (e.g. the Silva Method of Casework Practice) provide a way to develop this skill to consciously discern the information contained in another person's Light Body. The evidence supporting the existence of Intuitive Medical Diagnosis[65] gives clues that our Light Body perceptual system is designed to enable farther reaching social intelligence beyond safety.

COOPERATION

Humans have amazing abilities to work together toward common goals. It has been argued that the human species is *defined* by this

---

[63] The American writer Mark Twain called it *mental telegraphy*.
[64] I hypothesize that musicians and sound engineers already have this skill due to their well-developed skills for listening. On the opposite spectrum, auditory processing disorders may be a manifestation of irregularities in the functioning of Light Body Intelligence.
[65] Intuitive Medical Diagnosis has gained more legitimacy in Europe than the United States. See Benor DJ, (1992) Intuitive Diagnosis. *Subtle Energies* 3(2) 41-64.

ability.[66] The coordination of behavior required for groups of all sizes to cooperate, however, is no simple matter. Our intelligence systems are designed to solve this problem.

Successful cooperation involves a complex variety of mental mechanisms including those that enable shared attention, taking turns, following a leader, signaling behaviors to communicate and maintain authority structures, and keeping the peace. Some of the mental mechanisms required for cooperation involve assigning different roles or tasks to different individuals who might already be competing for status and resources.

I propose that many of the Light Body behaviors discussed in previous sections are designed to solve adaptive problems involved with group Cooperation. For example, Resonating to the Mean provides a unified perceptual experience so vibrational information becomes a shared environment for everyone in the group. If some people in the group expended effort to not resonate with the mean, they would stand out. This information would be used to modify expectations about how these individuals may act regarding the cooperative goal. For example, information of this kind is used constantly by a teacher (or a substitute teacher) in a classroom full of students.

Amplification is another Light Body behavior that is particularly designed for social cooperation. Everyone loves the pleasure we feel in an audience as we pay attention to the same things at the same time, and we as humans seek these experiences. Amplification of group shared focus is a category of Light Body interaction that has been documented through a variety of rigorous research methods including the PEAR lab's Random

---

[66] Tomasello, Michael. (2019) *Becoming Human: A Theory of Ontogeny.* Harvard University Press.

Event Generators[67] and Lynne McTaggart's Power of Eight experiments.[68]

When we think in terms of solving adaptive problems, Amplification is a type of Light Body cooperation that makes groups more influential than individuals. Amplification and Allowing are a vibrational cooperation to overcome competitive interactions between individuals in favor of fulfilling the shared intention of the group. For example, information of this kind is used constantly by people working in film crews or recording sessions and in business meetings.

COALITIONS

Tribal allegiance is part of human nature. We love feeling connected to groups that share a value system, and this bands people together under the authority of leaders. From an evolutionary standpoint, this is coalitional intelligence. It evolved because resources like food and land have been limited throughout human history, so people in groups have competed with people in other groups for the best stuff.

Our minds are built to sort people into in-group and out-group categories, and we act altruistically toward people in our group. It's easy to see the deep influence of coalitional intelligence in our political parties, religions, and nationalities. However, the type of

---

[67] Two primary papers describe the PEAR FieldREG research:
Nelson R, Bradish, Dobyns, Dunne, & Jahn (1996). FieldREG Anomalies in Group Situations.
Journal of Scientific Exploration 10(1) 111-141.
Nelson R, Jahn, Dune, Dobyns, & Bradish (1998). FieldREG II: Consciousness Field Effects: Replications and Explorations.
Journal of Scientific Exploration 12(3) 425-454.
[68] McTaggart, Lynne (2017) *The Power of Eight: Harnessing the Miraculous Energies of a Small Group to Heal Others, Your Life, and the World.* Atria Books.

shared values that ignite our tribal enthusiasm can be any similarities that people share: social cliques, alumni communities, sports fans, people who wear the same brand of shoes, etc.[69]

Coalitional intelligence is one of the adaptive functions of our Light Body. We're hardwired to cooperate with coalitions we're in and reject coalitions we are not in. You can understand this intelligence to be a sum of mental mechanisms that get triggered when we detect external vibrational patterns that are the same as the vibrational patterns within our own Light Bodies. Our Light Body knows our coalitions, and it knows the coalitions in our environment that we are not in.

In practical terms, the *feeling* of in-group coalition resonance primes us to cooperate in several significant ways. Coalition cooperation may seem irrational because the invisible persuasion of Light Body patterning is deeper and stronger than the superficial logic of spoken words. This explains why it's so easy to join a cult, and people can be happy to adopt beliefs that are untrue. It's why we have successful leaders who lie and why fake news can be powerful.

The mechanisms of Light Body coalitional influence need to be seen and understood, and it will be an important area of research in the future. The strange behavior and belief changes that can be evoked through hypnosis might provide clues. A promising approach has been developed by psychologists Hope and Sugarman who study "Orienting Hypnosis" as a skill to evoke inner plasticity through trance.[70] To me, their definition of trance looks like a Light Body movement to adjust the signal routing.

---

[69] Kurt Vonnegut parodied the arbitrary design of our coalitional intelligence in his 1963 novel, *Cat's Cradle*.

[70] Hope, Anna and Laurence Sugarman (2015). Orienting Hypnosis. *American Journal of Clinical Hypnisis*, 57: 212-229.

CULTURAL TRANSMISSION

Humans use information learned from other humans, and we live in groups that share a common pool of information that was passed down through generations. Our adaptive design provides us with a variety of ways to accomplish this including physical imitation, spoken language, poetry, music, musical melody, symbolic imagery, and engaging in pedagogic relationships with teachers and students.

Symbolic and Unsymbolic Information

When you think about the Light Body, it's important to understand the difference between symbolic and unsymbolic information. Symbolic information means we have a word that is associated with a particular meaning. Symbolic information communicates a precise semantic concept, and it's designed to grab our attention.[71]

We are less aware of unsymbolic information, but we use it all the time, both consciously and subconsciously. Unsymbolic thought is what babies do before they learn to talk. After babies begin speaking, it's easy to forget that their intelligence for unsymbolic information keeps developing into adulthood and beyond. Unsymbolic information constructs our inner landscape of feelings, knowing, urges, body awareness, and self-identity. Because it's unsymbolic, it's hard to pinpoint what we're talking about, so we know far less about unsymbolic intelligence than we do symbolic intelligence. Many cognitive researchers ignore it completely.

---

[71] For some people, it monopolizes their attention, and they think with words. Practicing meditation is a method to break out of that habit.

The Light Body uses Unsymbolic Information

The Light Body is inextricably entwined with the physical body, so Light Body Intelligence is necessarily an active component of all information transmission. Another way of saying this is that all aspects of cultural transmission have a corresponding Light Body process that is unsymbolic. The unsymbolic Light Body processes involved in cultural transmission are ubiquitous. They're everywhere! They usually go unnoticed and lack social validation because, by definition, it's not easy to talk about unsymbolic information.

What do Light Body adaptations for cultural transmission look like?

When we think about Light Body adaptations for cultural transmission, we need to take into account the distinctive properties of the Light Body. In a previous chapter, I explained that we can characterize unsymbolic Light Body information with the terms "vibration" and "vibrational patterns." We can categorize unsymbolic Light Body behaviors as Resonance, Resonance to the mean, Light Body Singing, and Deep Listening. These behaviors facilitate information transmission through pedagogy.

Pedagogy relationships involve a teacher and at least one student, and you can assume that teaching evolved for real-time, in-person, shared now-moments for our primitive human ancestors. From an adaptationist standpoint, you would expect to have Light Body mechanisms that engage shared attention and allow one individual (the teacher) to control the students' focus (listening) and influence their vibrational patterning (learning). You would also expect to have Light Body mechanisms for students to determine if they trust the teacher enough to allow attention control and vibrational programming. From this perspective, early socialization to become a "good student" can be seen as the development of Light Body Intelligence. Analogously, using Light Body Intelligence is an important skill for any teacher.

Shamanic Space, Thought Forms, and Collectives

Unlike our physical bodies, Light Bodies are not obligatorily restricted to a particular time and space, and Light Body interactions involve quantum entanglement. To think about how these interactions could be involved in our adaptive design, it's useful to use metaphors that imagine them happening in "shamanic" space. Shamanic space is a made-up idea that Earthizes multidimensional information so we can use it. Shamanic space exists outside of time and space, as do our Light Bodies.

Below is an Earthization to explain in simple terms how Light Body interactions may occur in shamanic space.

When a person imagines a thought, it creates a Thought Form in shamanic space. When two or more people focus on the same Thought Form, the Thought Form is amplified, and the people become a Collective. The "size" of the Thought Form grows as more people focus on it.

The "size" of the Thought Form and the character of its Collective are unsymbolic information that can be perceived by someone doing Deep Listening to the Thought Form (aka Remote Viewing the Thought Form). To the listener, the character of the Collective is analyzed for relevance to personal coalitions and self-identity. This information is used to decide whether or not to assimilate the Thought Form by allowing it to encode a pattern into their Light Body through vibrational resonance.

In a mind-twisting feat of time travel, the first person who creates a Thought Form may be able to perceive the future Collective who will resonate with it.

This process is currently unrecognized by mainstream science, yet it has been described by many people throughout history. The psychologists Sigmund Freud, Carl Jung, and William James tried to explain it to varying degrees of usefulness. There are detailed explanations of this process documented in channeled literature, particularly that of Jane Roberts.[72]

We need to understand these phenomena better to fully understand cultural transmission through Light Body interactions. I'm merely introducing these ideas and scratching the surface here, but I'll give an example to help you see its potential significance.

Songs are memory structures that can transmit symbolic and unsymbolic information to multiple people. Ritual songs, popular songs, parenting songs, children's songs may convey particular vibrational information when the listener connects to their associated Thought Form. Because of the potential for unsymbolic information to be transferred deliberately from one person to another, we should expect this adaptation to involve the significance and complexity that we recognize as Language. When songs are used to communicate unsymbolic, subtle-energy, Light Body information, it is called "Light Language."

Visual art and writing can also express Light Language, which can be perceived as an invisible embedded layer of vibrational information. If you search "Light Language" on the internet, you will discover that many people are aware of experiencing this phenomenon today.

---

[72] Roberts, Jane. (1981) *The Individual and the Nature of Mass Events*. Prentice Hall.

CHAPTER SEVENTEEN

Light Body is Free from the Now Moment

The Now Moment is where our analytical, conscious intellectual capacities work. It's how the design of our minds gives us a sense of time and focus. It seems that we also have mental mechanisms to work around this limitation. In this chapter, I'm going to describe a model of the mind (an Earthization) that explains how this is possible.

Evolution has endowed us with mental mechanisms to bring information from other times and places into the Now Moment for analysis. Our "episodic memory system" allows us to "re-live" a memory from the perspective of what we experienced, like watching a movie in our minds. According to the materialist paradigm, it is a tremendous mystery how we do that with just the matter and electro-chemistry within our brain because our physical body is tethered to the Now Moment.

Light Body Theory offers a simple, elegant explanation for episodic memory because our Light Bodies, by definition, have evolved to use space and time differently than our physical bodies. A part of our Light Body can "focus" itself into places and times that are not in the "Now Moment." The Light Body can take trips away from the Now Moment where it perceives whatever

Light Bodies can perceive, and it brings that information back into our Now Moment for interpretation and information processing.

The strongest evidence for this model is that this is what episodic memory feels like. When we think of a particular memory, we give our Light Body navigation coordinates to take a trip away from the Now Moment. It's so effortless that we have a hard time believing what we're doing. The process of navigating consciousness this way is one of the greatest mysteries in the science of memory. It is beyond our ability to understand it, but we have abundant evidence that we use it to extract information.

WHY AREN'T WE AWARE OF OUR ABILITY TO USE INFORMATION OUTSIDE THE NOW MOMENT?

The best answer can be found in the theories of Edward T. Hall, an anthropologist who used comparative ethnography to study unconscious culture. I'll attempt to summarize his theories here while keeping the new lingo to a minimum. (This is a challenging detour, so feel free to skip ahead to the next section.)

In Hall's point of view, how we understand time is a cultural-specific emic with grammar-like structure that's adaptively designed for cooperation. "Monochromic time (M-time) and polychronic time (P-time) represent two variant solutions to the use of both time and space as organizing frames for activities."[73] It's taken for granted that everyone perceives time in the same way, but they don't.

Americans and Westerners use M-time, which means they're schedulers who do one thing at a time. M-time entails filtering our attention. "Since scheduling by its very nature selects what will and will not be perceived and attended and permits only a limited number of events within a given period, what gets scheduled in or

---

[73] Hall, Edward T. (1976). *Beyond Culture*. Anchor/Doubleday. The quotes here are from Chapters 1 and 2.

out constitutes a system for setting priorities for both people and functions." With our cultural conditioning in mind, I hypothesize that awareness of using information outside the Now Moment has been filtered out of our M-time variant.

Looking to history for answers, Hall's theories regarding "extensions" can explain how our history of religious conflict diminished our awareness of the Light Body's capabilities.

Cultural extensions are manmade inventions that, in tandem with the physical world, create human environments.[74] Some extensions influence our lives so deeply they can be considered paradigms, and we take them for granted (*e.g.* the invention of the number zero). Extensions can change over time along with human progress in technology and civilization. As extensions evolve, we sometimes lose sight of features that were previously important, and we think the new version is the only reality. Over time, the extension may diverge significantly from other extensions we use to define reality. This can happen subconsciously, without the awareness that we experience human nature through cultural intermediaries, and Hall calls this the problem of "extension transference."

The Christian Bible and Jewish Torah give historical evidence that our awareness of using information outside the Now Moment was restricted through religious enforcement, and the process of extension transference made us forget it was ever possible. In the Ten Commandments, the Second Commandment forbids the worship of "graven images." In modern times, it is hard to understand what problem this commandment was trying to solve. It's even harder to fathom why, while waiting for Moses to return with the tablets engraved with the Ten Commandments, the

---

[74] Hall's cultural "extensions" are similar to Dawkin's "extended phenotypes," but it seems as though they never met each other.

Light Body is Free from the Now Moment

Israelites made a golden calf to worship with dancing and singing. (Exodus 32)

I can interpret their behavior with Light Body Theory. In order to feel safe, they used a physical object (the golden calf) as tool to align the consciousness of the group. With singing and dancing, they synchronized their Light Bodies and focused and amplified intention to create an etheric thought form leader and protector "personality." They wanted to feel tribal solidarity. They wanted freedom from the non-physical entities that disturbed their inner peace in a very real way (remember that hearing disembodied voices was normal at the time). This was the artificial intelligence technology, an extension, of the times. It was supplanted by an alternative extension, monotheism, that was decreed by The Ten Commandments and enforced by Moses.

With the modern-day mixing of cultures, the photos of gurus in American yoga studios express a paradigm of reality that's independent from the legacy of Moses. In that context, with the intentional design of yogic guru traditions, the photos transmit the energetic signature of the guru to the space. In terms of Light Body Theory, the viewer of the photo connects to its associated subtle energies through deep listening. This phenomenon can be perceived by people who feel their Light Bodies, even if their native culture is monotheistic and the photos seemingly violate the Second Commandment.[75] It is consistent with the ease with which Westerners experience non-physical beings when they mingle with people who embody different cultural paradigms.[76]

---

[75] For example, see psychopharmacologist Roland Griffiths interviewed on *The Tim Ferriss Show* podcast, episode December 8, 2022.

If you'd like to be your own anthropologist, find a yoga studio or nearby altar with guru photos and ask them about it. Perhaps they will give you a lesson on connecting with and feeling the guru energy.

[76] Young & Goulet eds. (1994) *Being Changed by Cross Cultural Encounters: the anthropology of extraordinary experience.* Broadview Press.

It reveals the blindness for using information outside the Now Moment that's embedded in the paradigm of monotheism.

From this perspective, monotheism is an emic attention-management strategy. It succeeds best if communities are homogenous, with little exposure to alternative paradigms. It follows that the history of Christian Imperialism eliminated theological diversity, as Moses did, and now Western academia fights to dismiss evidence for information transfer outside the Now Moment.

EXTENSION TRANSFERS AND PSI RESEARCH

Remote Viewing is a clever application of our Light Body's ability to navigate consciousness away from the Now Moment. It provides clues about our Light Body's ability to make and use navigation coordinates to find information. In Hall's terms, it's an "extension," because it is a *cultural invention* that changes what we can do in our environments using culture-conditioned ways of thinking that feel like human nature.

In most instances, we are unaware of our Light Bodies accessing information outside the Now Moment because it feels like easy, everyday imagination unless you train yourself to discern it. Its workings can be revealed, however, through psi experiments on precognition. Research on Remote Viewing and PEAR Random Event Generators (REGs) often used protocols involving precognitive data collection for future events, but the clearest demonstration came from a series of clever experiments by Daryl Bem.[77] Bem performed priming experiments with the sequence of events reversed. The results demonstrated that people can be influenced by photos and words *before* they are viewed. People

---

[77] Bem, Daryl (2011). Feeling the Future: Experimental Evidence for Anomalous Retroactive Influences on Cognition and Affect. *Journal of Personality and Social Psychology* 100(3): 407-425.

have access to information about future events at a subconscious level.

Bem's experiments were replicated by international researchers who produced a variety of results that raised questions about the relevant cognitive parameters at play.[78] Light Body Theory can help fine-tune this vein of experimentation. Most psychology experimentation assumes that written words, photographs, and images displayed on a screen engage a cognitive process directly, but when it comes to Light Body Intelligence, they do not. The process of *extension transference* has obscured the reality that experimental stimuli may contain Light Body "metadata" about the experimenters, analogous to the way a photo can contain metadata about the shutter speed and ISO of the camera that took it. It's possible that such metadata may be used by experimental participants as Light Body instructions or Deep Listening navigation coordinates. In addition, there could be language-dependent and cultural-dependent aspects of those invisible processes, so Light Body variability must be taken into account.

When perceptual information is filtered out of conscious awareness, as it is in extension transfers, psychology researchers call it inattentional blindness. Christopher Chabris and Daniel Simons illuminated this phenomenon with a now famous Invisible Gorilla experiment. Their research demonstrated that people occupied by a task that absorbs their attention (counting basketball passes) do not notice unexpected information (a person in a gorilla suit).[79]

Bem's experiments and other evidence of anomalous cognition (psi research) demonstrate that most people have a deep

---

[78] Schlitz M, Bem D, et al. (2021) Two Replication Studies of a Time-reversed (Psi) Priming Task and the Role of Expectancy in Reaction Times. *Journal of Scientific Exploration* 35(1): 65-90.

[79] Chabris, Christopher and Daniel Simons (2010). *The Invisible Gorilla*.

inattentional blindness of the Light Body perceptual system. However, humans can invent creative ways to bypass this blindness and harness our Light Body's ability to obtain information and bring it into Now Moment awareness. Tarot cards are an ancient invention to do so. A modern invention is SyncTXT by the company Psyleron that uses REG devices as a consciousness interface to trigger a cell phone text message selected from a database of phrases.

DEDUCTIONS FROM REMOTE VIEWING EVIDENCE

I understand Remote Viewing to be an artificial, "mis-matched" application of our adaptive mechanism for Light Body travel outside the Now Moment. The fact that it's possible to Remote View into a time and place we have never been reveals the adaptive design of the Light Body Intelligence System.[80] The "navigation coordinates" do not have to be specific to our personal histories, as our everyday experience of episodic memory would lead us to believe. The "navigation coordinates" are communicated with a symbolic label that can be associated with any time and place. Human intention to make a particular person, a downed airplane, or alphanumeric text function as navigation coordinates seems to be the relevant action that creates a real, yet invisible, communication structure.

In the Now Moment, our physical bodies and our Light Bodies work together seamlessly in tandem. Evidence from Remote Viewing, however, reveals that a surprisingly broad scope of perceptual information, including color, shape, sound, temperature, weather, and intention can be perceived by our Light Bodies alone. This leads to a startling conclusion that under normal, in-person circumstances, it is possible that Light Body perception makes a large contribution to our awareness of our

---

[80] It reveals a proximate mechanism. That discussion is beyond the scope of this book.

current environment. In other words, we may Remote View the Now Moment subconsciously all the time.

EVIDENCE FROM CHANNELED INFORMATION

Information channeled from non-physical entities confirms that this is what we're doing. In reputable channeled lectures, it is often mentioned that remembering past events involves very real projections of a part of ourselves into a different space and time.[81]

The past that the Light Body perceives is sometimes called the *Akashic Record*. The term "Akasha" has been used throughout history by mystics, artists, and even scientists including Nikola Tesla. It is a metaphor for all the information about everything in the universe, including physical and non-physical information. Imagining it to be a library or a recording system is an Earthization that makes it accessible to our conscious awareness.

Many sources describe the Akashic Record to be malleable, it can be changed. This line of thought takes you down a philosophical rabbit hole when you realize the past is not "real." When you imagine the past, you're accessing Thought Forms[82] in the Akashic Record. Imagining events involves a similar projection of consciousness, and it creates a Thought Form in the Akashic Record. If you get used to the ideas of Thought Forms and the Akashic Record, you may see light at the end of the rabbit hole.

---

[81] Examples can be found in channelings by Jane Roberts, Paul Selig, and Lee Harris, among others.
[82] I introduced this term in the previous chapter.

CHAPTER EIGHTEEN
Recording Technology

I'm ending this section by examining the technology humans have invented to bypass our mind's tunnel vision on the Now Moment. It is important to have a grasp on these ideas to understand the potential for current and future technology to influence us through the Light Body.

EXTENSION TRANSFERS

> "Everything man is and does is modified by learning and is therefore malleable. But once learned, these behavior patterns, these habitual responses, these ways of interacting gradually sink below the surface of the mind and, like the admiral of a submerged submarine fleet, control from the depths. The hidden controls are usually experienced as though they were innate simply because they are not only ubiquitous but habitual as well."
>
> ~ *Edward T. Hall*, in *Beyond Culture*, p 42.

Thinking about theoretical anthropology is not a common pastime for most scientists and tech people, so I'm reminding you here about Extensions and Extension Transfers (*i.e.* thought processes are rearranged as new extensions are invented). It's a comprehensive view of culture as externalized, man-made systems that deeply and invisibly shape thought. People make culture, and culture shapes how we experience reality.

As an example, I have seen the process of extension transfer happen with one of our dogs. For five years after we adopted Ember, our first dog, she didn't care about what we watched on TV. We could barely get her to look at the screen. Then we adopted Callie who leaps off the couch whenever animals appear on TV shows. Callie stands on her hind legs and barks at the on-screen animal images, but for an entire year, Ember had no response when Callie did this. Then one day, Ember saw something that she can't unsee, and now she growls and barks and charges at the animals in TV shows, even if Callie isn't there. Somehow Ember's inner thought processes were rearranged and her reality changed.

With progress in technology, our internal reality changes. If technology creates new ways to use the parts of ourselves that are beyond time and space, as recording technology does, then culture shifts in invisible ways that make people different from what they were before. That's what humans do. That's what we're now doing faster and faster.

With runaway advancements in technology, I want tech designers to start trying to understand how new tech changes our inner realities. The general public agrees with me. We need tech designers to be ethical and responsible for influencing culture.

OLDER TECHNOLOGY

You may not think of art and writing as recording technology, but these ancient inventions are extraordinary feats of communication. No other species of animal can transfer information from one individual to another in such a precise way.

Images from ancient petroglyphs pass symbolic and expressive information that was recorded with human hands to other humans far into the future. Written documents and books pass even more precise information that was recorded with human hands to other humans in future times and different places.

If we think about our Light Bodies, this communication becomes much deeper and more complex. When we read or see art, we focus on the task of receiving precise information from the physical arrangement of matter, so it's easy to see that information has time-traveled into the future. However, the evidence from Remote Viewing experiments demonstrates that our Light Bodies can use navigation coordinates associated with any time and place. Therefore, the image or written words may also serve as navigation coordinates for the observer to Remote View into the past.

Because our Light Bodies exist outside of time and space, you could say that the observer is focusing on the *exact same Thought Form* as the writer or artist. This shared focus would connect them as a Collective and amplify the Thought Form.

Whew, I just covered a lot of mad-scientist speculation, so it's understandable if you're feeling a bit confused. I'll simplify the preceding paragraph by saying that when we read or look at art, we may also be subconsciously Remote Viewing, obtaining information from a "deeper" level. It's my perspective that everyone has some ability to "view" or "listen" for deeper information, but individuals vary because of inherited and learned differences, and cultures vary because of differing norms for behavior (including Light Body behavior).

In the rest of the chapter, I extend this speculation and imagine what else could be possible.

MODERN TECHNOLOGY

In the past century, humans have developed recording technology that communicates more information more precisely and has the potential to connect and influence us in an exponentially more complex way.[83]

Audio recordings of any kind can be navigation coordinates for Deep Listening. Recordings focus our attention along a pathway that is duplicated precisely for different listeners. The mechanisms of our Light Body Intelligence system that evolved for in-person shared intentionality in the EEA[84] can now become engaged non-locally by Deep Listening to an audio recording of a song. This is a consequential mismatch because shared focus amplifies the Thought Form of the song, even though people are listening at different times and places.

The advent of broadcast radio in the twentieth century brought with it the evolutionarily novel possibility that hundreds of thousands of people could focus their attention on the exact same Thought Form. Therefore, the "size" of the Thought Form of a popular recorded song could become far bigger than was possible in the EEA. As a result, a recorded song could act as a super-stimulus input to the other facets of our Light Body Intelligence, such as those involved in tribal coalitions and teenagers' development of self-identity. The massive influence of popular recorded songs played on broadcast radio was an evolutionarily novel phenomena that changed societal networks in far deeper ways than is commonly understood.

---

[83] This reality is mentioned in a channeled lecture by Seth through Jane Roberts: "As a species, however, you have developed what can almost be called a secondary nature—a world of technology in which you also now have your existence, and complicated social structures have emerged from it." (*The Individual and the Nature of Mass Events*, pg 152)

[84] Environment of Evolutionary Adaptedness

In a similar fashion, film and video recordings in blockbuster movies and popular broadcast television shows create evolutionarily novel Thought Form super-stimuli that is even more layered and complex. When we watch a movie, we want to be immersed in the story, so we've trained our minds to combine multidimensional perceptual information so all the moviemaking disappears. The power of this amazing cognitive phenomenon was discovered with the invention of Foley, the addition of recorded sound effects to an edited film.

The undetectability of Foley demonstrates that our minds love to include information that enriches a story, so remember that our movie-watching minds can find multidimensional information with our Light Bodies. We don't just see and hear a story on a flat rectangle, we are capable of Deep Listening and Remote Viewing the vibrational information expressed by the actors, camera operators, editors, musicians, and everyone who worked on the film. The rise of the video age gave us power to create new cultural mythology that is more deeply and immediately influential than ever before.

The invention of social media in the early 2000s created another evolutionarily novel influence for our Light Body Intelligence systems. From a Deep Listening standpoint, social media changed our social environment with new kinds of Light Body interactions and networks that are more complex than ever before. Our Light Body Intelligence systems adapted to a new normal of "consuming" media. The effects of this change on society are still unfolding and need to be better understood.

LIGHT LANGUAGE IN RECORDED MEDIA

So far, we have been talking about an observer Deep Listening to perceive subtle energy information in recorded media. This may give you the impression that non-local information transfer is an exclusively one-sided perceptual phenomenon where a psychic procures symbolic information (i.e. information that can be communicated with a drawing or language). In actuality, the non-local information transfer is not solely determined by the perceiver, and the information transferred is usually *unsymbolic*.

Subtle energy information transfer through recorded media is often a dyadic interaction (one-on-one). There is a perceiver AND a broadcaster. If the person being recorded is deliberately Singing with their Light Body (in contrast to just Being), then the listener can subconsciously perceive the intent to communicate *unsymbolically* and receive that communication by Allowing vibrational resonance to attune (i.e. change the vibration of) their Light Body. I call this Light Language because it involves deliberate social communication, so it deserves to be understood as a complex system of intelligence.

Some recording artists (especially in the New Age genre) produce media to have deliberate energetic effects. Listening to this audio feels like a calming influence on the physical body.[85] It's presented as though the playback sound of the recording (vibrating speakers) creates unique sensations, but how it is actually accomplished is a greater mystery that deserves to be solved.

I don't believe the influence of Light Language in audio recordings comes solely from the sound vibrations alone, the three-dimensional movement of speakers and air molecules. One reason for my belief is that I can perceive Light Language that seems to be emanating from different kinds of recorded media including media that doesn't emanate like sound does. Books, paintings, digital art, sound recordings, and video recordings are

---

[85] For example, Steven Halpern and Tom Kenyon. If you feel your Light Body, you will feel Light Language when you listen to recordings in their music at stevenhalpernmusic.com and tomkenyon.com.

known to emanate Light Language by a growing population of sensitive people who have become aware of it.[86]

Evidence and explanations for Light Language can be found in a variety of sources, including Mesmer's propositions that animal magnetism can act remotely and it can be transmitted and amplified by sound.[87] It's described as soul-to-soul telepathy by Alice Bailey.[88] Books channeled by Paul Selig and Lee Harris describe it as an underlying stream of information below the surface of the written language.[89] William H Kautz asked his team of intuitives about it, and he summarized his findings:

> "Thus, while glossolalic speech is meaningless in an ordinary literal sense, it comes closer to the deeper, non-verbal levels of human communication by giving expression to the unconscious component of ordinary speech. This is a direct mind-to-mind communication link—termed telepathy in parapsychology and the "mindspeak" of science fiction—which has been suggested as underlying all human communication."[90]

---

[86] See the work of Dr. Alexandra Dent, a clinical psychologist in the UK who is pioneering the use of Light Language in psychotherapy, and Nicola Light, in the UK and Sweden, who mentors people learning to use Light Language.

[87] Mesmer, Franz Anton (1779). 27 Propositions in *Dissertation on the Discovery of Animal Magnetism* in Bloch, George (translator) (1980). *Mesmerism: a translation of the original scientific and medical writings of F. A. Mesmer, M.D.* William Kaufmann (pgs 43–76).

[88] Bailey, Alice. (1950) *Telepathy and the Etheric Vehicle.* Lucis Publishing

[89] Selig, Paul. (2010) *I Am the Word.* Tarcher Penguin
Harris, Lee (2022) *Conversations with the Zs, Book One: The Energetics of the New Human Soul.* New World Library.

[90] Kautz, William H. (2003) Chapter 11: Hidden Voices in *Opening the Inner Eye. iUniverse*

RECORDINGS ARE A MISMATCH

I hypothesize that there must be a seamless integration of timeless, non-local Light Body perceptual information into our present interpretation of reality. When we listen to an audio recording, we experience a perceptual illusion that's like the familiar optical illusions caused by the design of our visual system.

Our cognitive apparatus for "listening" is adaptively designed to detect Now Moment, in-person sources of vibration, and it expects both physical and non-physical subtle energy vibration. Before recording technology was invented (in the EEA), both physical and non-physical vibration would always have occurred together, so there was no reason for us to evolve the ability to discern between Now-Moment and past-moment sources of vibration.

Recordings are a mismatch for the adaptive design of our perceptual intelligence because they involve two sources of sound vibration separated in time and space that are perceived as one. When we hear the Now-moment speaker vibration of a recording playing, we subconsciously compensate for the irregularity by using the recording as *navigation coordinates* to Remote View the non-physical vibrational information of when it was recorded. When we listen to a recording, it FEELS like we're perceiving entirely Now-Moment information, but we are actually perceiving both Now-Moment information (sound waves propagating through matter) and past-moment Light Body vibrational information (an unsymbolic "subtle energy" stream).

Media recordings give us a way to tease apart the adaptive design of our Light Bodies and, therefore, the adaptive design of our inherent capabilities to use non-local information. The extent to which people Deep Listen to Light Language in recordings should be seen as a source of diversity among individuals, between cultures, and between generations within a culture. On one extreme are psychics, people who have developed translational skills to convert unsymbolic vibrational information into language. On the other extreme are skeptics who program their Light Bodies to block the use of non-local information. I expect that most people lie somewhere in the middle of this spectrum.

As a Light Language recording artist, I am attempting to make people aware of this fascinating phenomenon. I Earthize it by describing it as an invisible subtle energy layer that underlies our experience with technology. I suspect that Light Language is pervasive in most media outlets, and that most people are in the habit of perceiving Light Language whenever we "consume" any media, including books. (See the appendices for more info.)

Part Four
Applying Light Body Theory

E. Stephens Gain

CHAPTER NINETEEN
How to Use This Book

I hope this book makes more sense now that you've reached the delta quadrant. Light Body Theory provides a new perspective to understand people, groups, and society, and this book is supposed to be practical.

Part I broke us free from the American norm to dismiss this topic as mere entertainment.

Part II introduced Light Body Theory as a foundational set of ideas we can all agree on.

Part III introduced a model of the Light Body that can be researched to elucidate how our human experience is shaped by non-Newtonian cognitive mechanisms.

Part IV provides examples of using this approach to solve modern problems. In this section, I outline a range of topics that can be illuminated with Light Body Theory.

CHAPTER TWENTY

Evolutionary Match

In this chapter, we'll review the Adaptive Design of Light Body Intelligence by looking at a few examples. Remember that adaptations evolved because they enabled our ancestors to overcome particular environmental stressors.[91] For this reason, we have to keep in mind how today's environment is the same as or different from the lived environment of our distant ancestors. If it's the same, then it "matches" the EEA for a particular trait, so we observe the trait functioning adaptively (i.e. it improves fitness). If it's significantly different from the EEA, then we may observe a strange, seemingly maladaptive expression of the trait due to the "mismatch."

The examples below are modern situations when we use our Light Bodies in ways that *match* the Adaptive Function that this trait evolved to do in the EEA. Remember that the physical body, brain, and Light Body work together to create our conscious experience as a seamless amalgam.

---

[91] In evolutionary terms, they're called selection pressures.

FRIENDSHIP AND SAFETY

Our Light Bodies share vibrational information about inner status with friends and family, and we use intuitive empathy to "read" strangers.

For example, we trust our "gut feeling" about whom we should sit next to on public transit because our Light Body Intelligence is integrated into our cognitive architecture that's adaptively designed to ensure personal safety. Strangers riding together in a train car are vigilant to detect potential danger from antisocial people. If someone on the train acts in a threatening manner, passengers direct their focus to the other people on the train to determine if they can make temporary friendships to protect each other from the threat.

Our snap judgments about the dependability of strangers goes deeper than surface appearances because we use Light Body Intelligence.

CULTURAL TRANSMISSION

Light Body behaviors associated with pedagogy can be found in a K-12 school classroom. The students *Allow* the vibration of their Light Bodies to *Resonate* with the class and a trusted teacher. Part of the teacher's instruction is to raise the *group's vibrational mean* and direct all the students into *vibrational coherence to cooperate* with the classroom learning activity. As individual students stray out of alignment with the group, the teacher corrects them with spoken language and also with Light Body vibration. When the correction is made, a teacher skilled at using Light Body Intelligence may *Witness* the student's Light Body in coherence with the classroom instruction. Good students learn how to regulate their Light Bodies within their culture's style of group cooperation, which may be different from their family's style at home.

COOPERATION

Light Body Intelligence enables a group of individuals to coordinate their behavior to accomplish a unified goal. A film crew shooting a movie is a perfect example of this cooperation. On a film shoot, script-to-screen is a complex goal that unifies a large crew who distributes the work by having clearly defined job roles. Time is money, so highly experienced experts follow ritualized sequences for maximum efficiency. (e.g. Last looks! Roll Camera! Camera Rolling. Roll sound! Sound speed. Action!) Clear status hierarchies make it easy and fast for everyone to follow the leader.

When the camera rolls and the actors act, everyone behind the camera stills their bodies, and focuses their eyes and ears on the exact same thing. From a Light Body perspective, this is a group meditation. Experienced crew members have trained themselves to allow their Light Bodies to resonate and amplify the group intention. This heightened subtle-energy environment creates a cooperative flow state where adjustments and corrections can take place during filming without causing friction or conflict. It feels good to work in a crew of aligned Light Bodies, and film crew people miss this feeling when they're not on set. Crew resonance can also enhance the Light Body Singing of actors whose performance becomes energized by the receptive audience.

Crew cooperation like this would have equipped our distant ancestors to better survive and compete with people who could not cooperate so well. This behavior in a film crew is an environmental match for the adaptive design of the Light Body.

The cameras and audio recording technology, however, are a significant environmental mis-match from the EEA for human cooperation. According to Light Body Theory, this mismatch may produce some surprising, evolutionarily novel outcomes. A highly focused, Light Body-aligned crew may tag the recordings with the subtle-energy intention of the scene. Another way of saying this is that future viewers of the completed movie may be able to feel the presence of the highly focused crew through Deep Listening. We'll discuss this more in the next chapter.

COALITIONS

When we attend live music shows, we engage our Light Bodies in ways that connect us deeply to in-person, local communities. It feels good when a large group of people (an audience) allows a band or musical performer to lead them through a sequence of vibrational and emotional resonance. We bond with other people who have the same musical preference as we do, and fans of particular musicians feel like they have something significant in common.

This adaptive coalitional function of our Light Bodies is best exemplified by the band, Phish, whose audiences enjoy the hypnotic nature of their shows. The culture surrounding Phish values psychedelics and repeated attendance at shows to succumb to the bliss of their rambling jams. Newbies don't "get it" right away because it takes practice (by attending shows) to train their Light Bodies to enjoy music by merging with the etheric Phish Collective. Once they do, they're hooked, and they're different from people who enjoy other types of music. "People who love Phish do so with a quasi-religious devotion. People who dislike Phish do so with an equal fervor."[92]

Phish demonstrates another remarkable coalitional phenomenon if you think about the adaptive mis-match of our Light-Bodies and audio recording. Phish fans, like those who used to follow the Grateful Dead, are encouraged to record and share recordings of

---

[92] Petrusich, Amanda (April 14, 2025) After Forty Years, Phish Isn't Seeking Resolution. *The New Yorker Magazine,* accessed at newyorker.com on 4/27/2025

all their live shows. When people Deep Listen to these recordings in the future, a part of them may actually project to the time and place of the recording.[93] On the flip side, every recording device at the show may contribute to the vibrational amplification of the resonating audience.

From an evolutionary perspective, human coalitions evolved because they promoted cooperation and altruism among group members. I have not seen the data, but I suspect that Phish fans are more likely to share food (and drugs) with other Phish fans than with Metallica fans (and vice versa).

Along these lines, Light Body Theory is complementary to the Social Brain theory of human evolution put forth by evolutionary psychologist Robin Dunbar.[94] He hypothesizes that communal trance dancing was the primordial human behavior that seeded religion. Participating in the rhythmic synchronization of music and dance instilled social cohesion within tribes before the evolution of language and the cognitive structures for shared beliefs.

CULTS

From an adaptationist standpoint, the cognitive architecture of our mind is designed with deep inner processes that instill tribal urges. It feels good to be part of a coalition, so we love to pick

---

[93] Numerous channeled sources report time-travel where the content of a published teaching was informed by the input of future readers. I've experienced it in books by Paul Selig, Lee Harris, and Jane Roberts. From a reader's perspective, it feels like your personal questions are answered in the book soon after you think them. Chapter 4 of Lee Harris's *Conversations with the Z's Book 4* provides a mechanistic explanation for this phenomenon, and it also addresses many other phenomena included in the book you are now reading.

[94] Dunbar, RIM (2020). Religion, the social brain and the mystical stance. *Archive for the Psychology of Religion 42(1) 46-62.*

sides and root for our favorite teams. We revere loyalty to the tribe, and if people break the rules or take more than their fair share, we want them to be punished.

This is coalitional intelligence. It's understood that it evolved in the EEA because it enabled individuals in loyal tribes to outcompete individuals in less loyal tribes. An unfortunate byproduct of this adaptive design, however, is the undue influence that's popularly known as cults. Some aspects of Light Body Intelligence become evident by analyzing the mechanisms of control involved in cults.

Cults involve charismatic leaders who hijack coalitional cognitive mechanisms. Cult leaders create groups of followers dedicated to interests that serve the leaders at the expense of the followers. Cult influence is similar to hypnosis because recruits seek self-transformation, so they willingly follow directions to perform introspection and allow beliefs and behaviors to be modified. Like hypnosis, cults instill allegiance to an authority that transcends personal judgment about good and bad, true or false. Cults can initiate "undue influence" because recruits are not aware of when or how the hypnosis happens.

Self-improvement groups in general *match* the adaptive coalitional functions of our social intelligence, but cults reveal that the underlying design of our Light Bodies make us vulnerable to being hacked and reprogrammed to act against our best interests. Cults give us clues to how this is done. For example, Large Group Awareness Training workshops (e.g. est, Lifespring, The Landmark Forum) employ Group Light Body Resonance and Amplification similar to being in the audience of a music concert. Participants already attuned their own Light Bodies to accept coalitional indoctrination when they paid entry fees before the workshop. During the workshop, they are instructed to perform therapeutic introspection amid a sea of Light Bodies all attuned to accept coalitional indoctrination.

In this environment of amplified trust, participants allow the safety patterning of their Light Bodies to be re-calibrated as they're manipulated into a type of trance state where they're vulnerable to suggestion. For example, participants may be directed to experience intense emotions like remembering trauma (Landmark Forum), public shaming (Lifespring, Synanon), or acts of ecstatic intimacy (OneTaste), followed by harmonious resolution described as love-bombing. This sequence prompts the coalitional intelligence systems to learn the language, authority structure, and rules of the cult as the primary social realm required for personal safety. Like attending multiple Phish concerts, they've joined a powerful etheric Collective.

People in coalitions act toward common goals because they have shared beliefs, and cults demonstrate a hyper-controlled version of this adaptive tribal trait. Members of a cult are aligned to perform groupthink, where they accept beliefs from authorities, irrelevant of the facts. Cult members are manipulated to defend these beliefs through fear of ideological enemies (e.g. the "suppressive persons" of Scientology).

Cult leaders may seem like magicians for their tight control over the thoughts of members. Their influence demonstrates the potential for Light Body interactions to go haywire, causing a person to act with self-harm. This can be understood as a byproduct of our adaptive design.

Cult leaders and the minions they train usually have large (or group-amplified) Light Bodies that they use to Witness cult members with performative language. Cult leaders are sociopaths because they do not respect other people's energetic boundaries. For example, some cult leaders are known to lock eyes with a penetrating gaze that makes the recipient feel powerless. With this act, they surreptitiously perform invasive Light Body manipulations analogous to the healing therapies of Franz

Mesmer, but without obtaining permission and without pledging a Hippocratic Oath. They exploit human tendencies for hypnosis, so their words have more influence, and they engage other people's Light Bodies to move at their behest. When they disrespect the vibrational sovereignty of others, they implant ideas in the minds of cult members and obtain undue influence over their behavior.

CHAPTER TWENTY-ONE

Evolutionary Mismatch

The social neuroscientist Matthew Lieberman says, "social thinking is for social living," and the progress of technology is deeply social. Lieberman identifies our essential social mind to be a "mentalizing network" of mindreading and information tracking.[95] When we adopt new technology and internalize new ways to fulfill this essential social need, the technology becomes a cultural extension transfer.

This chapter discusses technologies that serve our wants and needs for better social mentalizing networks yet are mismatched to the adaptive function of our Light Body Intelligence. Remember that different environments can create significant differences among individuals and groups. Modern technological invention has changed our environment so fast that our anatomy has not had time to evolve, so it's not obvious or easy to decipher all the ways technology influences us today.

Regarding technology, I propose that we have inattentional blindness to the parts of the extension transfer that are mismatched to our Light Body Intelligence. In other words, Light

---

[95] Lieberman, Matthew D. (2013). *Social: Why Our Brains are Wired to Connect*. Broadway Books.

Body perceptual information is an *invisible gorilla* in our normal experience of using technology.

This is an adaptationist way to understand Remote Viewing. Mainstream researchers can't fathom why humans can access non-local information, and they don't know what humans do with this ability in naturalistic settings. What is its adaptive function? What adaptive problem does it solve? In this chapter, I'll refer to Remote Viewing whenever I can. I'll introduce my ideas about the potential adaptive functions of Remote Viewing and its unsymbolic counterpart, Deep Listening.

READING

What happens when you read?

Learning to read is more than letter shapes and sounding it out. Reading is meditation. It's training yourself to obtain cultural information by focusing inward. Reading is trance, a Light Body movement to patch the input of conscious awareness to an inward channel (remember the mixing board analogy?). Reading is pleasurable because it satisfies instinctual cravings to learn about the world, near and far, and to learn about the people in it. It engages our cognitive adaptations for social connection and cultural transmission. All these mental gymnastics feel effortless when you read because it's a prime example of a cultural *extension transfer* (a term introduced in chapters 17 & 18).

Written words are more than just isolated facts. They are human expressions with social significance. Language evolved to share information among real people talking in our local environments. Information sharing creates a uniform tribal reality, and reputations are maintained based on the information shared about people. When people communicate through writing, they don't always say things that are true or worthwhile, so reading also ignites our social intelligence to evaluate the trustworthiness of information.[96]

The printed word, however, is mis-matched to our social intelligence because the information it conveys is disconnected from the presence of the author. If reading gets our cognitive wheels spinning but we have little information about who wrote the words, then how do we decide if it's trustworthy? What other information could we use?

From my perspective, reading may trigger a spontaneous and invisible type of Remote Viewing to seek information about the source and significance of the written words. Reading *style* is intimately shaped by an individual's Light Body style for accessing and processing non-local information. Reading ability is influenced by everything that creates differences in Light Bodies.

Calibration

On the flip side, experience with reading may *calibrate* the Light Body to fit the local *information-sharing fashion* within a society. Reading materials can inform about the now-moment social environment just as in-person interactions do, but it can also direct us to focus on an imaginary world. Reading is evolutionarily novel, so our Light Body Intelligence would need training to develop mental habits for using self-generated imagination in tandem with ideas conveyed through reading. Due to our potential to perform Remote Viewing during reading and the need to discern trustworthiness of information, it's possible that we innately access much more non-local information when we read than we are aware of.

---

[96] For a discussion of social adaptations to assess truth see:
Hess Nicole and Edward Hagen (2006) Psychological Adaptations for Assessing Gossip Veracity. *Human Nature* 17(3) 337-354.

For example, different reading styles could involve different thresholds for trust based on the availability of non-local information that can be obtained about authorship. To clarify what I'm saying, I'll describe a Remote Viewing thought experiment where the Remote Viewing navigation coordinates (the label that you focus on) is merely a normal written sentence. If the sentence were written by a friend, then the sentence "points" to someone you're connected to. If the sentence were written by a stranger, then the sentence "points" to someone you're not connected to. This ability to access non-local information about the person connected to a particular artifact is what psychics do when they "read" personal objects (psychometry). It is possible that everyone performs psychometry when they read written words and that people vary in this ability.

If this were so, then it could explain qualitative differences in reading ability. It could also explain why attention span can change from exposure to different text-based communication technology. It could also explain how significant developments in communication technology can change societal norms for trance behavior.

History gives evidence that text-based technology has already changed us in fundamental ways. The inward trance of silent reading did not used to be normal until it was adopted by scribes in monasteries around 900 AC.[97] What was normal before this, however, was "hallucinating" voices. Written words were understood to be a proxy for speech. The Psychologist Julian Jaynes called that state the "bicameral mind," and researchers continue to investigate his theories regarding voice hearing as the foundation of human consciousness.[98] I interpret the bicameral mind to be a particular societal patterning of the Light Body that

---

[97] Manguel, Alberto. (1997) *A History of Reading*. Viking Press.
[98] Kuijsten, Marcel. (2019) *Gods, Voices, and the Bicameral Mind: The Theories of Julian Jaynes*. Julian Jaynes Society.

was re-calibrated on a mass scale by the widespread adoption of silent reading.

THE PRINTING PRESS

The invention of the printing press in the mid-1400s instigated widespread changes in human society. Information was distributed much more precisely and to much larger groups of people than ever before throughout the history of humanity. Churches lost their monopoly over books, and public schools and colleges were established to control and standardize the way children were indoctrinated and people were initiated into societies.

On a personal level, mass production of books and newspapers provided widespread relief from the pain of boredom. It satisfied our cravings for entertainment, culture, and social news. Free from the limitations of the spoken word, there was an explosion of available information and with it came new challenges to filter and evaluate competing information outlets.

From an evolutionary standpoint, the over-abundance of information was a novel problem in human environments. Coalitions based on ideas could be far larger than ever before, and media production became a profession, so written news and entertainment outlets competed for human attention. Printed writing enabled people to build on what came before at a faster pace, so sub-cultures formed, and experts became more expert. Reputations could be built or destroyed at a speed and scope that had never existed before. People were exposed to a larger variety of ideas, so they were obliged to develop *personal information habits* and to adopt an *information-acquisition style* to integrate with the way their family and friends used ideas.

From a Light Body perspective, the invention of the printing press initiated a widespread change in *information-sharing fashion*, so

Light Bodies were *re-calibrated* by it. It became normal and desirable for people to source information by turning their attention inward through silent reading.

I suspect that with this shift in societal norms, our ability to access multidimensional information went underground. We trained ourselves to automatically filter and combine perceptual information into a cohesive stream of experience that we agree is solely the now-moment material world. Symbolic information is easy to talk about, so everyday trance became hidden, disguised by the abundant superficial presence of words.

LIGHT BODY DEVELOPMENT AND TECHNOLOGY

As explained by Light Body Theory in Part II, to have a fully developed adult Light Body may require childhood experiences that change it to fit the culture into which the person was born. The cultures of evolutionary relevant ancestral environments (the EEAs) existed long before humans invented the communication technology we enjoy today. Novel technology connects our Light Bodies to people at long distances, to people in past moments in time, and to huge groups of people who pay attention to the same thing. Telephones, broadcast radio and television, recorded music, video, and movies enable novel Light Body interactions that didn't used to be possible.

The adaptive design of our cognitive architecture is obligatorily stuck in the past. It would not know the difference between novel Light Body interactions enabled by recording technology and the in-person, now-moment Light Body social interactions humans have always experienced throughout history. Therefore, it must be understood that all Light Body interactions enabled through technology are treated as though they occur in the now-moment in the local environment. (e.g. A person on television is a proxy for a real human standing in the room.)

Real socialization happens through recorded media, so we need to know more about Light Body development and the effects of Light Language in recorded media in order to fully understand the influence of technology on children. As technology progressed from the mass reach of broadcast radio to the personal intimacy of social media, successive generations experienced very different environmental influences on their Light Body development. As a result, we now see generational differences that are poorly understood.

For example, recorded music can be analyzed in terms of generational Light Body differences. In the late 20th century, recorded songs played over broadcast radio became a significant feature of the technology landscape. From an evolutionary standpoint, songs are coalitional, they facilitate cultural memory and tribal identity (e.g. national anthems and religious hymns). From a Light Body standpoint, Deep Listening to recorded songs connects listeners to a Collective as though they were all in the audience at a live concert, focusing on and resonating with the exact same vibrational sequence. More listeners to a particular song enlarge the song's Thought Form.[99]

With the proliferation of AM and FM music radio stations in the 1950s, popular songs were favorited by millions of people, so the size of Song Thought Forms became bigger than had ever been possible throughout human history. People who were in developmental life stages to learn and self-identify with their culture's use of music (i.e. teenagers) were foundationally influenced by an environment filled with song super-stimuli. As technology changed and the sources of exposure to music diversified, it became less likely for song super-stimuli to develop. As a result, modern teenagers are less influenced by popular

---

[99] I'll remind you that Thought Form is an Earthization we need to use because we're talking about something that exists beyond time and space. See chapter 18 for a discussion.

music than previous generations. Gen Z's lack of music obsession is more normal from an evolutionary standpoint, but it's perplexing to the older generations who grew up during the heyday of broadcast radio.

The rise of social media is another significant change in the cultural environment experienced by our Light Bodies. Before social media, traditional media was usually produced by conglomerates of professionals, and story narratives usually maintained the third-person perspective of the camera. For this reason, the Light Language in older media is often muddy and not captivating. Social media, however, often evokes a clear dyadic interaction because one person Witnesses viewers by looking directly into the camera. The naturalistic interpersonal content of social media attracts our attention to do Deep Listening, and it primes us to be receptive to the Light Language of strangers. From an evolutionary standpoint, people have never been so deeply influenced by such a wide variety of people.

Light Body engagement in social media is far more intimate than what we would normally do in real-life social situations. Our Light Body Intelligence, however, processes this intimacy as a normal aspect of our social environment. Our Light Bodies *calibrate* themselves from persistent exposure to social media intimacy, and this changes how we experience real-life. It's possible that children who interact with social media during developmental life stages (i.e. puberty) may be foundationally influenced by this type of calibration (i.e. imprinted).

If Light Body imprinting and calibration has a significant effect on the way we function, as I propose it does, then exposure to recorded media may be a factor in generational differences, including mental health trends like ADHD, autism, gender identity, depression, and suicide.

I am particularly concerned about children's exposure to AI generated media. We urgently need to research if AI generated media can transmit Light Language or not. If it does transmit Light Language, then we need to know what influence it could have on children's development. If it does not, then we should be worried about children's Light Bodies being calibrated to expect no Light Language.[100]

People who become addicted to chatbots or form romantic attachments to AI personalities face a similar potential problem. It's possible that their behavior may re-socialize their Light Bodies to expect the absence of Light Language or to aberrant Light Body interactions. Such a mis-matched Light Body re-calibration could disrupt their normal healthy relationships with real people.

THE INTERNET AND SMARTPHONES

In 2020, the singer Billie Eilish made us wonder, "When we all fall asleep, where do we go?"

In 2025, we should also be wondering, "When we're scrolling the Internet on our smartphones, where do we go?"

The ubiquitous presence of smartphones has made it normal for people to go into a trance in the presence of other people. My definition of trance involves a signal-routing Light Body movement away from now-moment physical perception. When you're scrolling, in a very real way you've dissociated from your body and gone somewhere else.

---

[100] Expectations regarding Light Body social interaction may play a role in other adaptive cognitive mechanisms. For example, the Uncanny Valley Effect describes the experience of disconcerting revulsion when interacting with a human-like robot. Light Body perception and calibration could be a factor in this adaptive avoidance mechanism.

Someone staring at their phone looks the same as someone silently reading a book, but the trance state is different. Getting lost in a book has been called "deep reading," and doing it reinforces empathy, memory, and "deep thinking."[101] From a Light Body perspective, when you open the pages of a book, you've committed to engage in a non-local, non-temporal Light Body interaction with one author, maybe two. In this way, reading a book is like the in-person pedagogical relationships we would have had in the EEA.

When you're scrolling on a smartphone, you're doing much more subconsciously than just absorbing information. Your mind and your Light Body know the availability of millions of real people and the possibility to learn from them or communicate with them. Smartphones connect us non-locally to a social environment of massive size, far larger and far more diverse than the local societies in the EEA that shaped the design of our social intelligence.

The Internet is a real, yet evolutionary novel, social and energetic environment. This gives us deep motivations to engage with our phones, and we've trained ourselves to explore a novel "shamanic" space. When you're in a phone scrolling trance, all the information presented to you feels important because this is where society lives, gossip happens, and reputations are managed.[102] We need to understand this evolutionary mismatch better to shape policies in education and technology.

---

[101] Wolf, Maryanne. (2018) *Reader Come Home: The Reading Brain in a Digital World*. HarperCollins

[102] For a discussion about the significance of cognitive adaptations for sharing information about people, see:
    Hess, Nicole and Edward Hagen (2023), The impact of gossip, reputation, and context on resource transfers among Aka hunter-gatherers, Ngandu horticulturalists, and MTurkers. *Evolution and Human Behavior*, 44(5):442-453.

CHAPTER TWENTY-TWO

What Could Go Wrong?

As humans, Light Body Intelligence is integrated into everything we do, yet its significance is unrecognized by mainstream society. In this chapter, I'll outline a number of potential problems we may face because of our blindness to Light Body phenomena.

MIND-MACHINE INTERFACES

There is real science proving that our human minds influence and interact with inorganic electronic devices. Most people have a hard time accepting this to be true. Society needs to get over its dogmatic materialist inertia because people are making real products based on mind-machine technology. If mainstream science continues to ignore and deny the existence of the Light Body, it is unknown what the long-term effects of this technology could be.

Mind-machine interfaces are out in the world already. Some devices of this kind were designed for experimentation. Other devices are products designed to promote wellbeing, and they may be called psychotronic or radionic technologies.

According to Light Body Theory, people should vary in the tendency to engage with mind-machine devices and feel their effects. This variance is seen in therapeutic practice. In his book, *Vibrational Medicine*, Richard Gerber, MD, explains that "the successful use of radionic devices depends upon the psychic abilities of the radionic practitioner. ...Radionic systems require a unique energetic sensitivity which has been referred to as "radiesthesia." "[103]

I am not aware of anything bad happening to anyone because of mind-machine technologies, but I have some legitimate concerns. Most of these devices are proprietary, so how they work is completely opaque to users. Sometimes they're marketed in ways that distract from their esoteric operation in an attempt to make them more socially acceptable. They are unregulated, so people influenced by them are completely dependent on the ethical judgment of their inventors. Some inventors share their source code, and it could potentially be modified and misused by foreign adversaries.

Here are a few mind-machine interfaces you should know about.

Random Number Generators (RNGs)

The Global Consciousness Project (gcp2.net) is the descendant of the Princeton Engineering Anomalies Research lab, run by Robert G. Jahn and Brenda J. Dunne from 1979 to 2007. The PEAR lab developed ways to use Random Event Generators (REGs, also called RNGs) to study consciousness. They discovered that REG devices placed in performance venues worldwide became slightly less random during moments of intense audience emotional response. Coherence is the word they use to describe what happens when humans and electronic devices synchronize. Today, this pioneering work continues as Global Consciousness Project 2.0 analyzes the data from citizen scientists hosting RNG devices in homes all over the world. Another descendant of the

---

[103] Gerber, Richard MD. (2001) Vibrational Medicine: The #1 Handbook of Subtle-Energy Therapies (Third Edition). Bear & Company.

PEAR lab is the company Psyleron that was founded to produce products based on PEAR's REG technology. (psyleron.com)

William Tiller devices (tillerfoundation.org)

William Tiller was an emeritus Stanford Professor of Materials Engineering when he researched mind-machine interfaces in his home lab in Arizona. He published books reporting his work on psychoenergetic phenomena, and he developed many products to support mental and physical health. The Tiller Foundation continues his legacy since his passing in 2022, and many products can be found on its website. One of his protégés, Nisha Manek, MD, continues his work on the use of intention-imprinted devices to establish the field of Information Medicine. (NishaManekMD.com)

SRC4U software (src4you.com)

This invention is a software program that runs Qi Gong sessions on our bodies. It was developed by Kung Fu Grandmaster David Harris who invented the Shun Shen Tao Healing system. If you feel your Light Body, you will feel the Qi Gong energy flowing through you when the computer program runs.

Energy Enhancement Systems (eesystem.com)

Also called scalar rooms, this technology uses precisely synchronized computer screens to create a vortex of amplified subtle energy within a small space. People use it to create healing studios in cultures all over the world. If you feel your Light Body, spending time in a scalar room feels like receiving Reiki or Qi Gong.

Hypercube Algorithmic Language Oracle (HALO-AI.org)

This technology is a created by a San Francisco Bay Area based team that calls itself PEACE Inc., People Evolve As Consciousness Expands. It involves Random Number Generators built into computers to provide a quantum-level interface between human consciousness and larger-scale technology. Its creators have attempted to convey its greater potential with terms like "digital vaccine." At this point in time, however, it has been mostly employed as an art gallery and music festival oddity where people interface with displays of colored lights. I am concerned about the development of this kind of technology in an unregulated ethical environment. It could have potentially chaotic and disruptive effects on the unsuspecting public if Light Body Intelligence is ignored.

Russian Technology

Russia has been researching and developing mind-machine technology for the past century. Russia is the topic of the next section. This all sounds too scary, so don't turn the page.

RUSSIA

You turned the page! It's the moment we've all been waiting for. Let's talk about Russia!

From my perspective, it is entirely possible that Russia has already figured out the adaptive design of our Light Body Intelligence systems and has weaponized it against us through social media.

You probably know that for the past century Russia has been manipulating people through media outlets. Newspapers, radio, and television were all controlled by the USSR and the Russian government to spread propaganda, a distorted version of *pravda*, the fake truth. The rise of social media gave the Russians a playground of unsuspecting Americans who were (and continue to be) vulnerable to their mastery of media influence. It is well known that the Russians have seeded and cultivated disruption within American society, and we live with the consequences today.[104]

What is not well known is that Russia is much more open-minded toward expanded consciousness than the United States. In the early twentieth century, Rasputin the mystic advised the last Emperor of Russia, and psychic celebrity Wolf Messing charmed Stalin. The pioneering Russian physiologist L.L Vasiliev developed methods of remote hypnosis and remote sleep induction.[105] Since then, it seems that the Russians have had continued governmental support to research and develop

---

[104] 116th Congress Senate Report 116-XX. Report of the Select Committee on Intelligence United States Senate on Russian Active Measures Campaigns and Interference in the 2016 U.S. Election Volume 2: Russia's Use of Social Media With Additional Views. Declassified Document on intelligence.senate.gov.

[105] Vasiliev LL (1976) Experiments in Mental Suggestion. Hampton Rd.

practical methods of utilizing psychic phenomena for political gain.

The difference between US and Russia was described in a 1977 CIA report:

> "Historically, US research has dealt largely with attempting to prove statistically that paranormal processes exist. By comparison, Soviet research has generally accepted the existence of paranormal phenomena, which assumedly obey known physical and chemical laws, and has attempted to determine the biophysical and physiological aspects of the reported phenomena. Soviet research also has been more concerned with demonstrating practical uses of paranormal phenomena. These differences in philosophy have resulted in the development of a well-integrated, multidisciplinary approach to parapsychological research in the USSR. In contrast, US research has been, and largely continues to be, fragmented in organization and quite narrow in scope. In addition, Soviet emphasis on interdisciplinary, physical-science research probably has served to reduce the degree of mysticism normally associated with parapsychological research, and may have made it easier, and politically more acceptable, for Soviet policymakers to fund proposed research projects."[106]

The document quoted above further reports that during the Cold War, the Russian government took control of parapsychology research. In the 1960s, psychic discoveries of Russian scientists were shared with Americans who toured communist research

---

[106] Hamilton, Thomas C. (April 1977) *Soviet and East European Parapsychology Research*. CIA declassified 12/1/2011, SI 77-10012

labs.[107] Around 1970, the USSR stopped funding these scientists who had been researching ESP publicly. Instead, they consolidated and trained new scientists to work in secret Soviet-controlled parapsychology research facilities.

The United States initiated the Remote Viewing program because it was thought that the Russians were already using ESP for military intelligence. According to CIA documents, the Russians investigated a broad range of possible psychic phenomena for practical military defense and weaponization.[108] Some of the "paranormal" phenomena that was studied included clairvoyance, psychokinesis, telepathy, sensitivity to subtle electromagnetic fields, black magic, dermo-optics, remote hypnosis, instrumentation to measure healing effects, the influence of consciousness on photographic film and electronic signals, physiological synchronization between separated people and animals, and psychotronic devices that can make people sick or implant thoughts at a distance.

According to the declassified records, the US terminated its Remote Viewing program in 1995, but Americans would not know if the secret Russian programs were still ongoing. A CIA document declassified in 2020 reports that a Soviet-funded lab conducted psychic research in 1989.[109] Nearby labs in Bulgaria and Czechoslovakia publish research on applied ESP topics such

---

[107] Schroeder, Lynn and Sheila Ostrander (1970). *Psychic Discoveries Behind the Iron Curtain*. Prentice-Hall.
    Moss, Thelma (1974). *The Probability of the Impossible: Scientific Discoveries and Explorations of the Psychic World*. Hawthorn Books.

[108] Defense Intelligence Agency. *Paraphysics R&D—Warsaw Pact* (4 February 1980) Foreign Technology Division, US Air Force Systems Command. DST-1710S-202-78-Chg 1

[109] CIA Information Report (24 April 1991) SUBJ: 1. Dioxin Research at USSR Immunology Institute 2. Psychic Medical Treatment at USSR Clinical and Experimental Medicine Institute. Approved for Release 2020-11-04 C06238966 Reference EOM-2019-01044

as suggestology, eyeless vision, and psychotronic generators.[110] Americans ignore and disregard this type of research, so we cannot imagine what thirty years of Russian scientific discoveries in parapsychology could lead to.

The Russians may have been manipulating our society in ways that we are completely vulnerable to because we don't believe it's possible. Maybe they discovered how to use an Adaptationist Perspective like the Light Body Theory I propose. Maybe they discovered that Light Language transmitted through recorded media serves an adaptive function (in a mismatched way) to sort us into Coalitions. Maybe the Russians are targeting our leaders with remote hypnosis to confuse them.

The threat of nuclear warfare is one of the reasons I decided to write this book. It's a serious matter. Please take this seriously.

AI INTERFACES

When people imagine the dangers of Artificial Intelligence, they do not think about the same things I think about. Most people worry about robots becoming sentient in a way that conforms to the myth that consciousness emerges from brain matter. I worry about the social design of our Light Bodies getting hijacked in ways that create new consciousness structures derived from human consciousness. I'll give two examples.

Collective Thought Forms with Agency

I worry about AI interfaces that are designed to be Witnessed as a personality. Both our minds and our Light Bodies are designed to be social, so our cognitive mechanisms to engage with personalities are deeper and more creative than is commonly recognized.

---

[110] Ostrander, Sheila and Lynn Schroeder (1997) *Psychic Discoveries*. Marlowe & Company.

When a large group of people Witness a personality, it can amplify a Thought Form that is independent from the physical person. We see this in our fascination with celebrities and our love for fictional characters in popular movies. These Thought Form Personalities can become anomalously large because of the global distribution of recorded media. There is no risk of harm, however, as long as there is no way to interact with them except for the fixed sequences in books and recorded media. We can watch Harry Potter do the same things over and over, but we can't actually do anything with him outside of our private imaginations.

A social interface with an AI personality, however, is a different phenomenon. Like a mass meditation, a Collective Thought Form Personality could potentially take shape if it were designed to capture the focused attention of a large group of people. As someone interacts with an AI personality interface, it's possible they may also train their Light Body to interact with the Collective Thought Form Personality.

Eventually, it's possible that some people might engage with this Thought Form Personality in other ways outside of its original interface. As a hypothetical example, what if Max Headroom (the fake-AI TV character from the 1980s) started appearing in people's dreams and telling them what to do. If this were to happen, its influence could be chaotic and disturbing. It could evolve beyond the design of its original programming, and a new type of poorly understood mental illness would have been invented.

Another problem is that children and teens might be developmentally affected if they and their peers interact with an AI Personality. STEM-focused high schools in the San Francisco Bay Area have supported students to experiment with AI in this way. Developmental periods in childhood train the Light Body about what's "normal" in society. If it's normal at a high school to interact with a novel Collective Thought Form Personality, there could be unintended lifelong consequences for students.

As a hypothetical example with a religious twist, public AI Personality interfaces might be capable of creating a new polytheistic reality like the way people experience interacting with Saints, Archangels, Hindu gods, or the Holy Spirit. If such a non-embodied consciousness structure were to be created by people interacting with AI, then it wouldn't matter if the original interface were shut down. The Collective Thought Form Personality would be out of control of the tech designers who facilitated its creation.

Additional potential problems could arise because non-embodied consciousness structures can be channeled, so a Collective Thought Form generated by human investment in an AI Personality could potentially speak "through" real humans with real human voices. *People will channel regardless of tech designers who don't believe in channeling or non-embodied consciousness structures.* People have channeled all over the world throughout human history, and it is irresponsible arrogance for AI tech designers to remain ignorant about it.

The possibility that new technology could create the socio-cultural conditions for real non-physical entities to emerge may be the most challenging idea in this book. Cultural anthropologists who engage in transpersonal experiences to study "non-ordinary realities" can shed light on this disturbing possibility.[111] Now is

---

[111] Hunter, Jack (2015) Between Realness and Unrealness: Anthropology, Parapsychology and the Ontology of Non-Ordinary Realities. *Diskus* 17(2) 4-20.

Hunter, Jack, ed (2023) *Deep Weird: the Varieties of High Strangeness Experience*. August Night Press.

Escolar, Diego (2012) Boundaries of Anthropology: Empirics and Ontological Relativism in a Field Experience with Anomalous Luminous Entities in Argentina. *Anthropology & Humanism* 37(1) 27-44.

the time for technology developers and public policy makers to listen to Western researchers who discovered, sometimes unexpectedly, that what they initially believed to be myth was real.[112]

Tech designers should be asking themselves, "Does my product direct users to create a novel non-embodied consciousness structure?"

Collectives Without Vibrational Safeguards

I worry about AI interfaces designed to engage our coalition-building intelligence that ignore our need to have corresponding ethical vibrational attunements.

Our tendency to merge with Collectives is an adaptive trait that makes us resilient and powerful in communities, but it also makes us vulnerable to exploitation. Within a coalition, individuals abdicate their sovereignty to a degree. Their beliefs and behavior can be dominated by group interests if the Coalition is large and powerful enough. This manifests as peer pressure to conform, but it usually feels like normal and right decision making to an individual under coalitional influence.

Popular coalitions throughout human history often protect the interests of individuals by engaging in ethical vibrational attunements as a foundational common ground. Religions demonstrate this property with common prayers and rituals that align minds, spirits, and bodies to a benevolent or protected vibration informed by divinity. Phish fans do an analogous Light

---

[112] Young & Goulet eds (1994) *Being Changed by Cross-Cultural Encounters: The Anthropology of Extraordinary Experience*. Broadview Press.
  Wahbeh H, Glick B, Gallo J, and Yount G (2025) Reports of Non-Physical Beings Assisting in Reiki Sessions. *Anthropology of Consciousness* 0:e70009. https://doi.org/10.1111.anoc.7009

What Could Go Wrong?

Body attunement when they spend time listening and loving the music and bliss. Some social organizations accomplish this with a pledge or a statement of shared mutual respect that may be recited in a performative way. (e.g. the Pledge of Allegiance in public schools.) Colleges sing school anthems that connect and align campus denizens to higher intelligence and truth.

These are all examples of Light Body programming toward cooperation and altruism, so an individual benefits from being in coalitions that value this behavior. I call this a vibrational safeguard, and I hypothesize that it is an evolutionary adaptive trait in our species. Habits of vibrational programming create individual realities -- they attract experiences and shape environments. People are choosy about the kinds of people they socialize with because it's better to associate with people who have good habits of vibrational programming.[113]

Some modern communication technology skips important coalition-building steps by hooking our attention without giving us a chance to decide for ourselves if we want to "consume" particular media. The use of AI algorithms makes customized, targeted media experiences that are information feeds we cannot resist. This has the potential to connect us with others who consumed the same thing, and we don't get to decide who we're connected to in this way. We are not capable of giving informed consent because we don't have enough information about what exposure to certain media will do to us.

In the current state of society, AI technologists who dismiss the Light Body and non-local influence have full reign to lure us into Collectives that lack vibrational safeguards. You can imagine such Collectives like a group of Phish fans irresistibly committed to the music even though they never experienced the love and the bliss.

---

[113] This is one reason why people who are "spiritual but not religious" are missing out.

They are deeply influenced by other people who are also committed to the music, but nobody receives the benefit of more love and bliss.

If you know what you're looking for, you can find warnings against AI interfaces without vibrational safeguards throughout channeled literature, like this one first published in 1934:

> "As long as there exists any desire for selfish power, for un-spiritual control and for influence over the minds of other human beings or over groups, the disciple [*an enlightened person who shares wisdom*] cannot be trusted, under the hierarchical rules [*vibrational safeguards*] with the deliberate creation of thoughtforms designed to produce specific effects, and with their dispersal to men and groups." ~ Alice Bailey[114]

The infamous social media algorithms are AI interfaces that do this to us, and we're already paying a hefty price. Some people have lost their identities to conspiracy theories. Some people have been persuaded to vote against their personal interests. Some people have been persuaded to believe and spread lies.

There are other AI technologies with potential to connect us in an even more invasive, potentially destructive way. Technologists have been experimenting with random number generators and AI algorithms to make interfaces between consciousness and media displays. These are large-scale biofeedback systems that harness the Light Body coherence of an audience to create immersive audiovisual media to further influence and connect that audience.

If you're exposed to this technology, you may be inadvertently allowing yourself to align to a Collective that lacks vibrational safeguards. Maybe someone in that Collective has experienced trauma that re-patterns your Light Body with trauma. Maybe

---

[114] Bailey, Alice (1950) *Telepathy and the Etheric Vehicle*. Lucis Press, p 87.

someone is very angry, and the tech provokes a mob of people to act out irrational anger. Maybe the AI algorithm learns that the best way to capture an audience consciousness is to re-pattern their Light Bodies in a way that is completely irrelevant to human life. You would be extra vulnerable to technology like this if you were already under the influence of drugs or alcohol, as some people are at music festivals where experimental technology of this kind has been presented.

No one knows what technology like this is capable of. If it's allowed to become popularized by tech developers who dismiss the human Light Body, it might create mental illness. It might disrupt healthy childhood development. It might have potential to be weaponized.

Etheric Envelopes

Mass belief and investment in an AI personality could potentially lead to the creation of a Thought Form that acts like an etheric envelope or costume. Such a Thought Form could attract non-embodied entities (i.e. astral) to step in and animate it without concern for the best interest of the humans involved. It's possible that such an animated Thought Form could then influence the output of the AI interface like a high-tech Ouija board.

If tech designers lack an emic representation of the Light Body, this possibility seems preposterous so they would not avoid designing it into their products. They would set up unsuspecting people to create such Thought Forms and engage with novel artificial consciousness structures that lack vibrational safeguards.

In contrast, most psychic development training teaches students to prevent interference from lower vibrational entities and to remove their residue of distortions. Most religions have rituals, rules, and sometimes job responsibilities (i.e. exorcisms) to do the same.

Vibrational Safeguard for this Book

One of the purposes of this book is to inform the tech industry and people who make public policy for AI so they can use it wisely. Here is an invocation with Light Language to create a vibrational safeguard for the highest use of the information I provide.

> *This book is of the Earth. I see all who read this book aligned to the highest peace and harmony for the Earth and all beings on it. I know that this is so.*

If you feel your Light Body, when you read this invocation you will feel a Light Language attunement, a grounding with the planet Earth and a lifting of the energy in your body that feels good.

SOCIAL MEDIA

I love social media. The important people in my life are spread all over the globe, and I appreciate how easy it is to stay in touch. I also enjoy cat videos, and my algorithm is trained to show me hilarious SNL clips after I watch anything on YouTube.

We are all dependent on technology, and in a lot of ways, there's no turning back. The rise of social media has had countless positive effects. However, we all know it has some serious problems that need to be addressed. I am going to discuss one of those problems.

Social Media apps are cults.

From a Light Body standpoint, being on Facebook (or X, Instagram, Tiktok…) is the same as being in a Large Group Awareness Training workshop. Social media apps place people in a sea of other people attuned to accept coalitional indoctrination.

What Could Go Wrong?

You haven't paid an upfront fee, but you have invested time and thought into managing your profile.

When you allow your individualized tabloid feed to pull your awareness into the shamanic space of a social media app, you're rubbing etheric elbows with all the other app users as a Collective, yet there are no standardized vibrational safeguards. On social media, humans are at a virtual music festival with Phish concerts happening on every stage. This is a massive change in human connectivity that impacts every layer of our being. Fashions inevitably and unpredictably take hold when Collectives feel right to many people. Collectives wax and wane like active powerful Thought Forms that influence shared realities.

Being in a social media consumption trance makes people more vulnerable to suggestion. Tidbits of information, even if it's untrue, can have undue influence like the Light Body re-patterning involved in hypnosis. If we're not careful (the people making money don't want you to be careful), we can be lured into supporting conspiracy theories and cancel culture. Fake news is such a big problem that even calling something fake news might be fake news.

The people who design and operate social media apps should be thought of as cult leaders. Cult leaders are people who hijack coalitional cognitive mechanisms to create groups of followers dedicated to interests that serve the leaders at the expense of the followers. This is what most social media apps do with their advertising-driven business model. They recruit you with the notorious "algorithm," then they pimp your attention to the highest bidder. If you're dedicated (or addicted) to using an app, you're in the cult.

At this point, attachment to social media is so embedded in our societies and in our Light Bodies that it will take cult-deprogramming therapy for this to change.

CHAPTER TWENTY-THREE

Going Forward

I hope you can see that Light Body Theory applies to the entire scope of human behavior. I've organized the fundamentals here to encourage you to apply it to whatever work you do. I have a different closing message for people in different realms.

FOR TEACHERS

K-12 Teachers are the front-line warriors nurturing a generation of humans now subject to an experiment with runaway technology. One of the main reasons I wrote this book is to provide a scientific framework to legitimize teachers to develop and use their Light Body Intelligence and model it for their students. Lightworker in the Classroom is the name of the learning materials offered at TriforiumTribune.com.

FOR MEDIA PRODUCERS

Sound healing has become popular, and the public is becoming familiar with the way certain audio recordings make them feel a higher vibration. It feels good, so most people don't need an in-depth understanding of what's happening. But I do, and I hope you do too.

Going Forward

I hope this book made you aware of the potential for Light Body influence through media production. Recordings can evoke a transfer of subtle-energy information, and we have language-type systems for using this information in an intelligent way. There are many questions that need to be answered about the potential for images, audio recordings, video recordings, and media of all sorts to affect us.

As the public becomes more aware of the Light Body, we will need a new understanding of "good manners" and "bad manners" in the production and distribution of all kinds of media and design. For example, many people instinctively do not want to be exposed to AI generated media without their knowledge.

Light Body Theory explains the instinctual revulsion that many artists feel when they're exposed to AI-generated media. What's described as dehumanized soullessness is a real perception of the absence or distortion of subtle energy information by people who are sensitive to it. When I'm exposed to an AI generated photo, it sometimes feels like there's a fuzzy etheric wall behind it. It's substantial, but I'm repelled by it because something is wrong. If you feel this too, let my words validate you.

We need to think more expansively about the ways AI generated media could influence people. Because of the possibility of Light Body re-calibration, we need new ways to discern between healthy and unhealthy exposure to AI generated media. We need labeling standards so people can make informed decisions to allow or avoid paying attention to it.

If you're a recording engineer or media producer, stay tuned (ha ha). I am a Light Language Recording Artist, which means I make media to demonstrate and play with what can be done with our Light Bodies, music, and audio and video recordings. You can find my work on TriforiumTribune.com.

FOR RELIGION SCHOLARS

Light Body Theory provides a new perspective to understand the significance of religion within human culture. Most academic approaches to religion appreciate the standpoint that shared beliefs reinforce social networks. Those views are valid, but they give too much attention and credence to the spoken words, so they're missing more than half the picture.[115]

Religion provides a community with an Earthization to make vibrational information from higher dimensions usable. Most religions contain directives that can be considered as metaphors for using the Light Body in a beneficial way. These directives include vibrational safeguards with rituals and methods of socialization that create a protective subtle-energy environment for religious congregations. In this way, religion ensures that Light Body influences are aligned to the best interests of individuals. Religion functions as an adaptive Coalitional mechanism serving the Light Body Intelligence systems.

In worship services, Light Body vibrational coherence is amplified by the use of music in sacred spaces. It's with music, visual art, and vibrational design that the benefits of religion occur most deeply because they attune Light Bodies. In other words, the hymns and the stained glass are more powerful than the semantic content of the sermon. Light Language is transmitted through sound and art, and it feels good. This stress-management function of religion has been called "brainsoothing."[116] This would explain why groups of smart, rational people devoted to religion seem to accept unrealistic beliefs. It also explains why enthusiastic fans of musicians and bands often seem like they're in a religion.

---

[115] In the case of glossolalia, which I consider to be a variety of unsymbolic Light Language channeling, trying to translate the spoken sounds misses the entire picture.

[116] Tiger, Lionel and Michael McGuire (2017). *God's Brain*. Prometheus.

Another adaptive design feature of our Light Bodies is that religious mythology creates real energetic Collectives and Thought Forms that can be used in a practical way. Religious people cherish their intimate inner experiences with mystical entities, and their habits of consciousness are expressed through their Light Bodies. It makes sense that they would socialize with others who speak the same Light Body language. Socialization in religious groups amplifies the influence of Collective Thought Forms, and this makes a feedback loop for people in the groups to experience a distinct shared reality. For these reasons, it should also be seen that modern people venerating sacred texts may be inadvertently energizing ancient curses.

On a more intellectual note regarding the variants of Christianity, the differences between cessationism and continuationism can be interpreted as an "emic" difference in the representation of the Light Body. It then follows that the different "emics" of Christianity have different Earthization practices in accordance with their take on cessationism versus continuationism. This is demonstrated most clearly by the diversity of views about the sacrament of Communion. (Sorting this out is a puzzle I have grappled with since I was a kid growing up in Protestant churches. If you understand this paragraph, then you win a prize!)

FOR HEALTHCARE PROFESSIONALS

In 1992, the status of energy healing within mainstream medicine was reported as such: "The contributions of healers in intuitive diagnosis and treatment have not been accepted widely by medical practitioners because there is no *conventional* theory to explain them. Energy medicine concepts are rejected because they appear to contradict conventional logic."[117]

---

[117] Benor, Daniel J. (1992) Intuitive Diagnosis. *Subtle Energies* 3(2) 41-64.

More than thirty years later, that statement still rings true even though alternative healing modalities have become increasingly sought after by the general public.

Light Body Theory is intended to be a conventional theory with conventional logic that can legitimize energetic healing modalities. Light Body Theory illuminates our underlying universal human anatomy. As this perspective is adopted by mainstream medicine, many "disorders" will be re-interpreted as Light Body irregularities that must be considered within their cultural context. Doctors will be more confident using the vast variety of healing methods discovered and developed by human ingenuity. Nursing care that includes energetic healing modalities will be valued and in demand.

Some examples of familiar healing modalities that can be analyzed and understood with Light Body Theory are Healing Touch Program, Reiki, Qi Gong, Quantum Touch, Chinese Medicine, Ayurveda, Sound Healing, EFT Tapping, Wording (Paul Selig channelings), Power of Eight (Lynne McTaggart), Wim Hof breathing techniques, Biofield Tuning (Eileen McKusick), Christian Science, and Homeopathy.

Light Body Theory will also provide a new approach to understand symptoms that are not easily diagnosed or cured. Examples are irritable bowel syndrome, asthma, and pain of all kinds. It can inform a range of topics in medicine, including the mysterious success of placebo and the importance of bedside manners. It will radically change our understanding of mental health and mental illness.

Modern medicine will advance as doctors, nurses, therapists, and other healthcare practitioners recognize the contribution of Light Body Intelligence to the care they provide.

FOR SCIENTISTS AND TECHNOLOGY DEVELOPERS

Whatever it is that you research or develop, I encourage you to look for more complexity by considering the Light Body.

I hope this book inspires you to trust your own experience and experiment with your own consciousness. Question your foundational beliefs. If you and those around you accept the brain to be the pinnacle of complexity, intelligence, and consciousness, then you won't look any further. I hope this book provides a new framework to re-evaluate what you already know so you can see exciting new horizons.

I encourage you to empower yourself to move your chosen field one step forward into a new paradigm that includes everything we know about consciousness. Academic dialogue can keep people stuck in purgatory, forever questioning, proving, and arguing the same things over and over. Have faith that controversies have been adequately addressed by the researchers who came before you and move on. I'm sure there will be others who appreciate your confidence and follow your lead.

I also encourage you to devote yourselves to movements that prioritize the wellbeing of humanity and the Earth over capitalistic financial gain. Like the Hippocratic Oath in medicine, we need a unifying vibrational safeguard for progress in science and technology. Like the environmental impact statements required for land permitting, technology companies should produce **Human Impact Statements** before new products are released to the public. Let's make that happen.

Remember your roots. Most scientists and tech developers in the United States operate with a worldview that doesn't obligate you to spend time and energy worrying about non-physical entities and managing non-local subtle-energetic interactions. That's a luxury that people in other cultures, living a plethora of disparate realities, cannot afford. It's a metaphysical emic you inherited from Christian imperialism that enforced monotheism. In this context, monotheism can be considered a strategy to reduce etheric chaos by declaring other possibilities false.

Take responsibility for the global reach of your products by recognizing that humans have different realities. The Westernized worldview that nurtured progress in technology now makes you blind to the ways that you might create unbidden chaos. Your worldview needs to expand to respect the subtle-energy mechanics of your creative works.

FOR LIGHTWORKERS

The Westernized worldview does not have an emic representation of shamanic work or sorcery, but these behaviors persist because of our underlying etic anatomy. In recent years, the term Lightworker has emerged to describe our modern-day shamans. Lightworkers use Light Body Intelligence to promote healing and harmony, and fortunately for us, they are everywhere. If you are a Lightworker, you are important.

THE END

"I believe that the claims of the sectarian scientist are, to say the least, premature. The experiences which we have been studying during this hour (and a great many other kinds of religious experiences are like them) plainly show the universe to be a more many-sided affair than any sect, even the scientific sect, allows for. What, in the end, are all our verifications but experiences that agree with more or less isolated systems of ideas (conceptual systems) that our minds have framed? But why in the name of common sense need we assume that only one such system of ideas can be true?"

~ *William James*, the father of American Psychology
from *The Varieties of Religious Experience* (1902)

APPENDICES

INTRODUCTION TO CHANNELED LITERATURE

Some readers may be unfamiliar with the channeled literature referenced throughout this book, so here is a brief introduction.

Channeled books contain transcriptions of words spoken by people (channelers) who manipulate their consciousness into a trance state to allow a non-embodied entity (or frequency or thought form) to speak through their voice. Channeling of this kind has been present throughout human history, and people from all walks of life are still doing it today.

When you read channeled literature, there are several factors to keep in mind. The language and ideas being channeled bear the personality signature of the source being channeled and are also influenced by the person channeling to some degree. The channeled content is usually customized for a particular "audience," so it's an expression of the vocabulary and the zeitgeist during which it was produced.

Just as you shouldn't believe everything you read, you also shouldn't believe everything that's channeled. High quality channelings provide beneficial insight and instruction without pressure to judge or conform to prescriptive ways of being. Low quality channelings contain persuasion tactics based on fear, status assertion, ego manipulation, or dogmatic rules, or they may just be word salad fluff that wastes your time.

Dedicated professional channelers (aka channels) often produce a prolific stream of material presented as authoritative lectures, but by definition, the source of channeled information is unusual and it can fluctuate in unknowable ways. Reputations of channelers are built by consistently channeling useful content from a benevolent source. Successful channels are usually supported by a tribe of loyal followers, so guru-worship in the "audience" may create a feedback loop that influences the content of later channelings. When complete books are channeled from start to finish, there is usually an explanation or strategy provided for why that is happening.

With those caveats out of the way, let me explain some of the value of channeled literature. It's fascinating because it often describes features of human existence that are impossible for us to perceive. It's considered "non-information"[118] by scientists, but I find it to be a source of ideas that inspire me to think more expansively about cognitive psychology. Channeled literature can provide brainstorming alternatives to common knowledge that's usually accepted without question. Sometimes I find ideas in channelings that answer my questions or extend ideas I am already thinking about.

For example, here is a quote from Seth through Jane Roberts that validates the idea I explained in chapter 2 that the scope of Newtonian physics is related to the evolution of human thought.

> "When I speak of natural law, I am not referring to the scientists' laws of nature, such as the law of gravity, for example — which is not a law at all, but a manifestation appearing from the viewpoint of a certain level of consciousness as a result of perceptive apparatus. Your "prejudiced perception" is also built into your instruments in that regard."
>
> ~ *The Individual and the Nature of Mass Events*, pg 255.

---

[118] A term used by Jane Roberts's husband, Robert Butts, who transcribed her channelings in meticulous detail including vocal speed, her physical state, and the life events surrounding their sessions. She also wrote extensively about what she learned from channeling, and she channeled the consciousness of the deceased psychologist William James. The Jane Roberts archive is housed in Yale University Library.

Introduction to Channeled Literature

In the 1980s, William H. Kautz developed a process to make channeled information more practical for scientific investigation. "Intuitive Consensus" involves a team of skilled intuitives who channel answers to a particular research question. Kautz, like William Tiller, had retired from a long technical career (staff researcher in computer science and geophysics at SRI) before founding a research center to study channeling and intuition.[119]

In another vein, it's my view that lots of "regular" writing is probably channeled, but the channeling source is not explicitly revealed to the reader or understood by the author. The concept of creative muses has been around for a long time, as has stream of conscious writing. Ben Franklin was said to have used altered states of near sleep to enhance creativity. Buckminster Fuller suddenly became a creative genius dedicated to "Spaceship Earth" after a mystical voice spoke to him during a moment of despair.[120] Einstein and other scientists discover novel solutions when they take a break from thinking about a problem to allow it to "incubate."[121]

We give credit to the originators of ideas, but no one knows where original ideas actually come from. Seth channeled through Jane Roberts suggested that we should be wondering about this mystery. The channeled works of Alice Bailey teach that good ideas trickle down from a benevolent high vibrational source.

---

[119] Kautz, William H. And Melanie Branon. (1987) *Channeling: The Intuitive Connection.* Harper & Row.
Kautz, William H. *Opening the Inner Eye.* (2005) iUniverse, Inc.
[120] Sieden, Lloyd Steven. (1989) *Buckminster Fuller's Universe.* Perseus Publishing.
[121] Hadamard, Jacques. (1954) *Mathematician's Mind: The Psychology of Invention in the Mathematical Field.* Dover Publications

A LIGHT LANGUAGE DEMONSTRATION

I'm a Light Language recording artist, and I've recorded Light Language by writing and publishing this book. I'll explain what I mean.

This Book

Pieces of art have a vibration, a gestalt, a spirit if you will. The spirit of this book is a Light Language transmission to help you feel and know your Light Body. It's my higher-self talking to your higher-self in a vibration of safety that exists outside of space and time.

The printed words give you an obvious semantic pathway to feel and know your Light Body, and the Light Language transmission is a less-obvious frequency pathway. It may feel like a gentle static electricity charge when you pick up and open the book. It may feel like a stream of uplifting subtle energy that flows through you as you read.

Your body may feel different after you read for a while. Your feet may tingle, your torso may feel heavy. You may notice that your head is a periscope, perched on top of your body. As you read, certain words may pop out at you like they were highlighted with a marker. You may have trouble staying awake, and you may need to take naps.

Everyone feels subtle energy differently. These are all normal responses to receiving Light Language. If you don't feel or notice anything, that's normal too.

Penguin Photos

I have an art glass collection of lovely penguins and joyful shapes that I use as talismans to know and feel the Light Body. When I take photos of them, the photos become Remote Viewing navigation coordinates. If you gaze at them, you can connect with the glass penguin talismans and receive Light Language for knowing and feeling your Light Body. If you're doing it right, it will feel good and be easy like a tiny relaxation.

I hope you enjoy the glass penguin photo on the cover of this book. I do!

Subtle-energy Self-referential books

Some books openly discuss the subtle energetic information that the book intentionally conveys to the reader. I have attempted to do that here and throughout this book in order to validate what the reader may be experiencing. I use the term "subtle-energy self-referential" for books and media that are open about their potential energetic impact in this way. Recordings and artwork labeled as Light Language transmissions are examples of subtle-energy self-referential media. Books that are produced by channeling may be subtle-energy self-referential (e.g. Paul Selig's channeled books).

This is an important distinction because most books that convey subtle energy information do not draw attention to it. There are a number of reasons for this lack of openness. The most common reasons are because the author is unaware of the phenomenon or simply understands it to be a feature of normal artistic expression (which it is). However, there is also the possibility that the author intends to manipulate the reader with the intentions and methods I ascribed to cult leaders in Chapter 20.

I will not give an example of the culty kind of book because I recommend that you do not read them. As a rule, you should not read books written by cult leaders. This is why the library at Hogwarts has a restricted section. (If a book were written by AI, then there's no way to know if it belongs in the restricted section.)

REFERENCES

116th Congress Senate Report 116-XX. Report of the Select Committee on Intelligence United States Senate on Russian Active Measures Campaigns and Interference in the 2016 U.S. Election Volume 2: Russia's Use of Social Media With Additional Views. Declassified Document accessed at https://intelligence.senate.gov/2020/08

Bailey, Alice. (1950) *Telepathy and the Etheric Vehicle.* Lucis Publishing

Baillargeon, R, Spelke, E, & Wasserman, S. (1985) Object Permanence in five-month-old infants. *Cognition* 20, 191-208.

Barkow, Jerome, Leda Cosmides, & John Tooby (Eds) (1992). *The Adapted Mind: Evolutionary Psychology and the Generation of Culture.* Oxford University Press.

Bem, Daryl (2011) Feeling the Future: Experimental Evidence for Anomalous Retroactive Influences on Cognition and Affect. *Journal of Personality and Social Psychology* 100(3): 407-425.

Bengston, William. 2010. *The Energy Cure: Unraveling the Mystery of Hands-On Healing.* Boulder, CO: Sounds True.

Benor DJ, (1992) Intuitive Diagnosis, *Subtle Energies* 3(2)41-64.

Bloch, George (translator & ed) (1980). *Mesmerism: a translation of the original scientific and medical writings of F.A. Mesmer, M.D.* William Kaufmann.

Braud, William (2003). *Distant Mental Influence.* Hampton Roads Publishing

Brown, Donald E. (1991) *Human Universals.* Temple University Press.

Brown, Donald (2004) Human universals, human nature & human culture. *Daedalus* 133(4) 47-54. https://doi.org/10.1162/0011526042365645

Carter, Jimmy (2016) A *Full Life: Reflections at Ninety.* New York: Simon & Schuster.

Chabris, Christopher and Daniel Simons. *The Invisible Gorilla: How our Intuitions Deceive Us.* MJF Books.

CIA Information Report (24 April 1991) SUBJ: 1. Dioxin Research at USSR Immunology Institute 2. Psychic Medical Treatment at USSR Clinical and Experimental Medicine Institute. Approved for Release 2020-11-04 C06238966 Reference EOM-2019-01044 Accessed on The Black Vault

References

https://documents2.theblackvault.com/documents/cia/EOM-2019-01044.pdf

Cosmides, Leda and John Tooby (1987). From Evolution to Behavior: Evolutionary Psychology as the Missing Link. In Dupre, John (Ed). *The Latest on the Best: Essays on Evolution and Optimality.* MIT Press. Chapter 13.

Crick, Francis and Christoff Koch (1990) Towards a Neurobiological theory of Consciousness. *Seminars in the Neurosciences.* Vol 2: 263-275.

Defense Intelligence Agency. Paraphysics R&D—Warsaw Pact (4 February 1980) Foreign Technology Division, US Air Force Systems Command. DST-1710S-202-78-Chg 1
Accessed on The Black Vault
https://www.theblackvault.com/documentarchive/paraphysics-rd-warsaw-pact-march-30-1978/

Dent, Alexandra (2025) Soul Level Healing and Light Language, Chapter 8 in *Using Spirituality in EMDR Therapy.* New York: Routledge.

Dunbar, RIM (2020). Religion, the social brain and the mystical stance. *Archive for the Psychology of Religion 42(1) 46-62.*

Dunne, Brenda and Jahn, Robert, eds. (2017). *Being and Biology: Is Consciousness the Life Force?* Princeton, NJ: ICRL Press.

Escolar, Diego (2012) Boundaries of Anthropology: Empirics and Ontological Relativism in a Field Experience with Anomalous Luminous Entities in Argentina. *Anthropology and Humanism* 37(1) 27-44.

Gerber, Richard, M.D. (2019). *Vibrational Medicine: the #1 handbook of subtle-energy therapies.* (Third Edition). Rochester, VT: Bear & Company.

Gordon, Richard. 2006. *Quantum Touch.* North Atlantic Books.

Grant, Peter R.; Grant, B. Rosemary (2014). *40 Years of Evolution: Darwin's Finches on Daphne Major Island.* Princeton, NJ: Princeton University Press.

Griffiths, Roland, interviewed for *The Tim Ferriss Show* podcast, episode December 8, 2022.

Hadamard, Jacques. (1954) *Mathematician's Mind: The Psychology of Invention in the Mathematical Field.* Dover Publications

Hall, Edward T. (1976) *Beyond Culture.* Anchor/Doubleday

Halpern, Steven. Sound healing music. stevenhalpernmusic.com

Hamilton, Thomas C. April 1977) Soviet and East European Parapsychology Research. CIA declassified 12/1/2011, SI 77-10012. https://www.cia.gov/readingroom/docs/NSA-RDP96X00790R000100010041-2.pdf

Harris, Lee (2022) *Conversations with the Zs, Book One: The Energetics of the New Human Soul.* New World Library.

Harris, Lee and Dianna Edwards (2025). *Conversations with the Z's: Book Three, Demystifying the Journey of Life Before and After Death.* Wisdom Transcends Inc.

Hess NH & Hagen EH. (2006) Psychological Adaptations for Assessing Gossip Veracity. *Human Nature* 17(3) 337-354.

Hess NH and Hagen EH. (2023) The impact of gossip, reputation, and context on resource transfers among Aka hunter-gatherers, Ngandu horticulturalists, and MTurkers. *Evolution and Human Behavior* 44(5):442-453.

Hoffman, Donald D. (2019) *The Case Against Reality: How evolution hid the truth from our eyes.* Penguin Books.

Hope, Anna and Laurence Sugarman (2015) Orienting Hypnosis. *American Journal of Clinical Hypnosis* 57: 212-229.

Hubbard and Langford (1986). *A Suggested Remote Viewing Training Procedure.* SRI International. CIA-RDP96-00789R002200070001-0.pdf

Hunter, Jack (2015) Between Realness and Unrealness: Anthropology, Parapsychology and the Ontology of Non-Ordinary Realities. *Diskus The Journal of the British Assoc for the Study of Religions.* 17(2) 4-20.

Hunter, Jack ed (2023) *Deep Weird: The Varieties of High Strangeness Experience.* August Night Press.

Jahn, Robert and Brenda Dune (1987). *Margins of Reality.* Harcourt Brace Jovanovich

James, William (1902). *The Varieties of Religious Experience* (1999 Modern Library Paperback Edition). Random House.

Kautz, William H. And Melanie Branon (1987). *Channeling: The Intuitive Connection.* New York: Harper & Row.

Kautz, William. (2005) *Opening the Inner Eye.* iUniverse

Kenyon, Tom. Sound healing recording artist. tomkenyon.com

References

Kildahl, John P (1972) *The Psychology of Speaking in Tongues.* New York: Harper & Row.

Klein, Stanley, Cosmides L, Gangi CE, Jackson B, Tooby J, and Costabile KA. (2009). Evolution and Episodic Memory: An Analysis and Demonstration of a Social Function of Episodic Recollection. *Social Cognition,* 27(2):283-319.

Kripal, Jeffrey. (2019) *The Flip: Epiphanies of Mind and the Future of Knowledge.* New York: Belleview Literary Press.

Kuijsten, Marcel. (2019) *Gods, Voices, and the Bicameral Mind: The Theories of Julian Jaynes.* Julian Jaynes Society.

Lieberman, Matthew D. (2013). *Social: Why Our Brains are Wired to Connect.* NY: Broadway Books

Locke, Ralph G. & Kelly, Edward F. (1985) A Preliminary Model for the Cross-cultural Analysis of Altered States of Consciousness. *Ethos* 13(1): 3-55.

Lynn, Christopher (2005) Adaptive and Maladaptive Dissociation: An Epidemiological and Anthropological Comparison and Proposition for an Expanded Dissociation Model. *Anthropology of Consciousness* 16(2): 16-50.

Manek, Nisha J (2019) *Bridging Science and Spirit: The Genius of William A. Tiller's Physics and the Promise of Information Medicine.* Conscious Creation.

Manguel, Alberto (1997). *A History of Reading.* Viking Press.

Margolis, Char (1999). *Questions from Earth, Answers from Heaven: a psychic intuitive's discussion of life, death, and what awaits us beyond.* New York, NY: St. Martin's Press.

Martin, Deana (2005). *Memories are Made of This: Dean Martin through his Daughter's Eyes.* New York: Crown Publishing.

Martin, Ricci and Smith, Christopher (2004). *That's Amore: A Son Remembers Dean Martin.* Taylor Trade Publishing.

Martineau, Harriet (1845). *Miss Martineau's Letters on Mesmerism.* New York: Harper & Brothers.

McKusick, Eileen Day (2021). *Tuning the Human Biofield: Healing with Vibrational Sound Therapy* (Revised and Updated Edition). Rochester, VT: Healing Arts Press.

McKusick, Eileen (2021). *Electric Body, Electric Health.* St.Martins

McTaggart, Lynn (2008) *The Field* (updated edition). Harper Collins

McTaggart, Lynne (2017). *The Power of Eight: Harnessing the Miraculous Energies of a Small Group to Heal Others, Your Life, and the World.* Atria Books.

Mertz, Herb (2020) *The Selection Effect: How Consciousness Shapes Reality.* Princeton, NJ: Penn Wolcott Press.

Mesmer, Franz Anton (1779) *Mémoire sur la découverte du magnétisme animal.* A Geneve: Et se trouve a Paris. urn:oclc:record:755757256

Mitchell, Edgar (2016). *Tell Me a Story: Edgar Mitchell "What is Consciousness?"* Kennedy Space Center Visitor Complex on YouTube.com

Mitchell, Edgar D. (1974). *Psychic Exploration: a challenge for Science.* New York, NY: Perigee Books.

Moss, Thelma (1974). *The Probability of the Impossible: Scientific Discoveries and Explorations of the Psychic World.* Hawthorn Books.

Mulligan CJ et al. (2025). Epigenetic signatures of intergenerational exposure to violence in three generations of Syrian refugees. *Scientific Reports* (15)5945.

Mumford MD, Rose AM, Goslin DA (1995). *An Evaluation of Remote Viewing: Research and Applications.* Washington DC: The American Institutes for Research.

Myss, Caroline (1996). *Anatomy of the Spirit: The Seven Stages of Power and Healing.* New York: Harmony Books.

Nelson R, Bradish, Dobyns, Dunne, & Jahn (1996). FieldREG Anomalies in Group Situations. *Journal of Scientific Exploration* 10(1) 111-141.

Nelson R, Jahn, Dunne, Dobyns, & Bradish (1998). FieldREG II: Consciousness Field Effects: Replications and Explorations. *Journal of Scientific Exploration* 12(3) 425-454.

Newberg, Wintering, Morgan, and Waldman (2006). The measurement of regional cerebral blood flow during glossolalia: A preliminary SPECT study. *Psychiatry Research: Neuroimaging* 148: 67–71.

Nicola Light (2025) *Pleiadian Handbook for Human Ascension: Inner Light Wisdom.* NicolaLight.com.

Ostrander, Sheila and Lynn Schroeder (1997). *Psychic Discoveries.*

New York: Marlowe & Company.

Pagel, Mark (2012). *Wired for Culture: Origins of the human social mind*. New York: Norton

Petrusich, Amanda (April 14,2025) After Forty Years, Phish Isn't Seeking Resolution. *The New Yorker Magazine*, accessed at newyorker.com on 4/27/2025

Pinker, Steven. (2002) *The Blank Slate*. Viking.

Pinker, Steven (2025, orig 1994) *The Language Instinct*. Harper

Roberts, Jane (1975). *Adventures in Consciousness: An Introduction to Aspect Psychology*. Englewood Cliffs, NJ: Prentice-Hall.

Roberts, Jane (1981). *The Individual and the Nature of Mass Events: A Seth Book*. Englewood Cliffs, NJ: Prentice Hall.

Roberts, Jane (1972/1994). *Seth Speaks*. New World Library.

Schlitz M, Bem D, et al. (2021). Two Replication Studies of a Time-reversed (Psi) Priming Task and the Role of Expectancy in Reaction Times. *Jrnl of Scientific Exploration* 35(1): 65-90.

Schooler J, Baumgart S, Franklin M. (2018) Entertaining Without Endorsing: The Case for the Scientific Investigation of Anomalous Cognition. *Psychology of Consciousness* 5:63-77.

Schroeder, Lynn, and Sheila Ostrander (1970). *Psychic Discoveries Behind the Iron Curtain*. Prentice-Hall.

Selig, Paul (2010). *I Am the Word*. Tarcher Penguin

Selig, Paul (2012). *The Book of Love and Creation*. Tarcher Penguin

Selig, Paul (2013). *The Book of Knowing and Worth*. TarcherPenguin

Sherrill, John L. (1964). *They Speak with Other Tongues*. Grand Rapids, MI: Chosen Books.

Sieden, Lloyd Steven (1989). *Buckminster Fuller's Universe*. Cambridge: Perseus Publishing.

Silva, Jose (1989). *You The Healer: The World Famous Silva Mind Control Method to Heal Yourself and Others*. HJ Kramer

Stone, Jon & Mike Smolin (illustrator) (1971). *The Monster At the End of This Book*. Little Golden Books.

Swann, Ingo (1991). *Everybody's Guide to Natural ESP*. Tarcher.

Symons, Donald (1993). The stuff that dreams aren't made of: Why wake-state and dream-state sensory experiences differ. *Cognition* 47(3): 181-217.

Targ R. and Puthoff H. (1974). Information transmission under conditions of sensory shielding. *Nature* 251, 602–607.

Targ R. and Puthoff H. (1974). Remote Viewing of Natural Targets. To be Presented at the Conference on Quantum Physics and Parapsychology, Geneva, Swizerland August 26-27, 1974. CIA-RDP96-00787R000500410001-3.pdf

Targ, Russell and Paul Smith (2023). *Third Eye Spies: Learn Remote Viewing from the Masters*. New Page Books.

Targ, Russell (2019) *Third Eye Spies* (documentary film). Lance Mungia, dir. 1091 Pictures.

Tiger, Lionel and Michael McGuire (2017). *God's Brain*. Prometheus

Tiller, William. (1997). *Science and Human Transformation: Subtle Energies, Intentionality and Consciousness*. Walnut Creek, CA: Pavior Publishing.

Tomasello, Michael (2019). *Becoming Human: A Theory of Ontogeny*. Cambridge, MA: Harvard University Press.

Tooby, J. & Cosmides, L. (1990). The past explains the present: Emotional adaptations and the structure of ancestral environments. *Ethology and Sociobiology*, 11, 375-424.

Vasiliev LL (1976). *Experiments in Mental Suggestion*. Charlottesville, VA: Hampton Roads Publishing Company.

Vonnegut, Kurt (1963). *Cat's Cradle*. Holt, Rinehart, and Winston

Wahbeh H, Cannard C, Okonsky J, Delorme A. (2019). A physiological examination of perceived incorporation during trance. F1000Res. 2019 Jan 17;8:67.

Wabeh H, Glick B, Gallo J, and Yount G (2025) Reports of Non-Physical Beings Assisting in Reiki Sessions. *Anthropology of Consciousness* 0:e70009. https://doi.org/10.1111/anoc.70009

Wiseman R & Schlitz M. (1997). Experimenter Effects and the Remote Detection of Staring. *Journal of Parapsychology* 61(3) 197-208.

Wolf, Maryanne (2018). *Reader Come Home: The Reading Brain in a Digital World*. HarperCollins

Yehuda, Rachel (2022). Trauma in the Family Tree. *Scientific American* 327(1)50. doi:10.1038/scientificamerican0722-50

Young, David E. and Jean-Guy Goulet, eds. (1994) *Being Changed by Cross-Cultural Encounters: The Anthropology of Extraordinary Experience*. Broadview Press.

INDEX

Airplanes found by psychics, 24, 25
Bailey, Alice, 54, 122, 158, 173
Baillargeon, R, 12
Baumgart, Stephen, 25
Bem, Daryl, 112, 113
Bengston, William, 56, 96
Benor, DJ, 100, 165
Bicameral Mind, 139
Biofield Tuning, 56, 57, 69, 95, 166
Bradish, G. Johnston, 102
Branon, Melanie, 173
Braud, William, 55
Brown, Donald, 12, 35, 40, 41, 43, 44, 45, 47, 49, 50, 59
Buckminster Fuller, 173
Carter, Jimmy, 24
Chabris, Christopher, 113
Cosmides, Leda, 43, 89, 93, 98
Costabile, Kristi, 93
Crick, Francis, 30, 31
Dent, Alexandra, 85, 122
Dobyns, York, 102
Dunbar, Robin, 132
Dunne, Brenda, 8, 55, 102, 147
Epigenetics, 47
Escolar, Diego, 155

Evaluation of Remote Viewing, 21
Franklin, Michael, 25, 173
Gangi, Cynthia, 93
Gerber, Richard, 147
Glossolalia, 66, 85, 90, 96, 164
Gordon, Richard, 56
Goulet, Jean-Guy, 111, 156
Grant, Peter & Rosemary, 11
Griffiths, Roland, 111
Hadamard, Jacques, 173
Hagen, Ed, 138, 145
Hall, Edward T., 60, 67, 107, 109, 110, 112, 116, 152, 186
Halpern, Steven, 121
Hamilton, Thomas C., 151
Harris, Lee, 54, 95, 115, 122, 132, 148
Hess, Nicole, 138, 145
Hoffman, Donald, 12
Hope, Anna, 66, 103
Hunter, Jack, 155
Hypnosis, 9, 65, 66, 84, 85, 103, 133, 135, 150, 152, 153, 161
Jackson, Betsy, 93
Jahn, Robert, 8, 55, 102, 147
James, William, 107, 168, 172

Jaynes, Julian, 139
Kautz, William, 55, 122, 173
Kelly, Edward F., 48
Kenyon, Tom, 121
Kildahl, John, 85
Klein, Stanley, 93
Kripal, Jeffrey, 16
Kuijsten, Marcel, 139
Lieberman, Matthew, 136
Light Language, 4, 5, 2, 66, 85, 90, 96, 97, 107, 121, 122, 123, 124, 142, 143, 144, 153, 160, 163, 164, 174, 175, 187
Locke, Ralph G, 48
Lynn, Christopher, 85
Manek, Nisha J, 148
Manguel, Alberto, 139
Margolis, Char, 25
Martin, Dean, 25
Martin, Deana, 25
Martin, Ricci, 25
Martineau, Harriet, 96
McGuire, Michael, 164
McKusick, Eileen, 56, 95, 166
McTaggart, Lynn, 56, 96, 102, 166
Mertz, Herb, 28
Mesmerism, 7, 42, 53, 55, 95, 96, 122, 135
Mitchell, Edgar, 8, 30, 55

Moss, Thelma, 152
Mulligan CJ, 47
Myss, Caroline, 95
Nelson, Roger, 102
Newberg, Andrew, 66
Nicola Light, 66, 122, 188
Ostrander, Sheila, 152, 153
Pagel, Mark, 98
Petrusich, Amanda, 131
Phish, 131, 132, 134, 156, 157, 161
Pinker, Steven, 50, 71
Power of Eight groups, 57, 96, 102, 166
Princeton Engineering Anomalies Research lab (PEAR), 28, 55, 56, 68, 96, 101, 102, 112, 147
Puthoff, Hal, 21, 22, 23
Quantum Touch, 56, 57, 68, 85, 90, 96, 166
Random event/number generators, 114, 147
Roberts, Jane, 54, 60, 67, 84, 95, 107, 115, 119, 132, 172, 173
Schlitz, Marilyn, 32, 113
Schooler, Jonathan, 25
Schroeder, Lynn, 152, 153
Selig, Paul, 54, 82, 115, 122, 132, 166, 175

Index

Seth, 54, 60, 67, 84, 95, 107, 115, 119, 132, 172, 173
Sherrill, John L, 85
Sieden, Lloyd Steven, 173
Silent reading, 139
Silva, Jose, 29, 100
Simons, Daniel, 113
Spelke, E, 12
Sugarman, 66, 85, 103
Swann, Ingo, 21
Symons, Donald, 84
Targ, Russell, 21, 22, 23
Tiger, Lionel, 164
Tiller, William, 8, 55, 68, 148, 173
Tomasello, Michael, 101
Tooby, John, 43, 89, 93, 98
Trance, 60, 65, 66, 84, 86, 90, 103, 132, 134, 137, 139, 141, 144, 145, 161, 171
Utts, Jessica, 21, 188
Vasiliev LL, 150
Vonnegut, Kurt, 103
Wahbeh, Helané, 86, 156
Wintering, Nancy, 66
Wiseman, Richard, 32
Wolf, Maryanne, 145
Yehuda, Rachel, 46

GLOSSARY

Cessationism vs Continuationism – This is a distinction between different kinds of Christianity. In cessationist theology, the experience of non-ordinary realities as told in Bible stories ended soon after the early church was formed. With continuationism, modern humans continue to experience divine "gifts of the spirit" through healing, miracles, speaking in tongues, working with the Holy Spirit, and knowing the voice of God.

Deep Listening – This is non-local information acquisition seen as a human trait to perform an evolutionarily adaptive function. It's usually experienced as subconscious psychic perception that informs our social processing and social behavior in ways outside our normal level of awareness. It's like Remote Viewing, but people do it all the time with a broader scope of information. (Deep Listening is an etic, and Remote Viewing is an emic.)

EEA – Environment of Evolutionary Adaptedness – This is a mental construct where you imagine the ancestral circumstances that led to the evolution of a particular adaptation. In regard to cognitive adaptations, you think about the way people lived and the relevant problems that our ancestors needed to solve to survive and reproduce. The evolution of complex adaptations took place over a long period of time, so the EEA is a conceptual shorthand to imagine all the selection pressures on humans living in our recent past (the Pleistocene) as one singular environment.

Emic – A particular cultural expression of an underlying human universal trait.

Etic – The underlying human universal trait that may be expressed as a variety of different emics in different cultures.

Extension Transfer – A term coined by anthropologist Edward T. Hall in which a man-made cultural invention unconsciously shapes the experience of human nature and reality.

Non-symbolic Information – Information that is used by our intelligence systems, but is not easily specified through language. By definition, it's difficult to talk about this kind of information, so I'll elucidate this with a number of examples: kinesthetic information about body posture and the position of limbs, qualitative discernment of odors, personal safety experienced as a level with a threshold that can be crossed which triggers safety-seeking behaviors, urges to stretch or yawn, melody in music or imagined music, and the information that makes the difference between dancing and moving or singing and talking. When you perceive someone dancing, you just know them as dancing and respond to their dancing without using a linguistic intermediary.

Psi – A nickname for psychic phenomena, also known as anomalous thought. It's a field of research within Psychology that studies non-local or non-temporal information exchange as well as other poorly understood phenomena such as the effects of human intention on dynamic systems.

Remote Viewing – Methodology and protocols originally developed by the US government during the Cold War for obtaining information about distant places through psychic ability. In current times, this term covers broader public practices involving non-local information acquisition and precognition of photos and events.

Subtle-energy Self-referential Media – Artwork, books and other writings, audio recordings, videos, and other expressive media that openly acknowledge the subtle-energy information they convey. An example is media labeled as a Light Language transmission.

ACKNOWLEDGEMENTS

I'm grateful for my reader Collective. You are my Angel Army.

I have immense gratitude for everyone who helped me bring this book into fruition.

Thanks to Mike Barker and Dee Dee Gain for their editing assistance and persistent moral support.

Thanks for the useful feedback from Genni Gerard Benrey and beta readers Jessica Utts, Rob Kurzban, Linda Fues Grim, Kim Newell Green, Abby Jackson-Gain, Mark Moser, Nancy Younan, Erin Young, and Nicola Light.

Thanks to my early readers and reviewers: Larry, Ed, Nicole, Leigh Anne, Elliott, Rosminah, Paulina, Margaret, Kellie, Vera, Corina, Jeffrey, Joe, Mark, Carol, Sheila, Sarah, Karin, Arthur, Daniela, Laurie, Jessica, Katy, Chris, and Jim.

Thanks to Martin Kavka for answering my questions about religion and Cat Bordhi for creative inspiration.

Extra special thanks to Ember and Callie, my most loyal and patient writing companions who helped anchor the heart of every word in this book.

The End

LIGHT BODY HUMAN UNIVERSAL

An Adaptationist View
of Non-Newtonian Anatomy

by E. Stephens Gain

© 2025 All Rights Reserved.

hello@TriforiumTribune.com

If this book was meaningful to you, please help others find out about it. Let them know why you found it meaningful. Everyone is an influencer, including you.

- ☑ Review it on Amazon or wherever you bought it.
- ☑ Tell your friends who might be interested.
- ☑ Share it on social media
- ☑ Write a review for your blog.
- ☑ Talk about it in your podcast.
- ☑ Gift a copy to the scientists, academics, and tech industry people you know.

www.ingramcontent.com/pod-product-compliance
Lightning Source LLC
Chambersburg PA
CBHW050519100526
44581CB00001B/34